MW00423508

Queer Rock Love

ALSO PUBLISHED BY TRANSGRESS PRESS

Now What?
A Handbook for Families with Transgender Children
Rex Butt

Letters for My Sisters:
Transitional Wisdom in Retrospect
Edited by Andrea James and Deanne Thornton

Manning Up:
Transsexual Men on Finding Brotherhood, Family and Themselves
Edited by Zander Keig and Mitch Kellaway

Hung Jury:
Testimonies of Genital Surgery by Transsexual Men
Edited by Trystan Theosophus Cotten

Giving It Raw:
Nearly 30 Years with AIDS
Francisco Ibañez-Carrasco

Love Always:
Partners of Trans People on Intimacy, Challenge, and Resilience
Edited by Jordon Johnson and Becky Garrison

Real Talk for Teens:
A Jump-Start Guide to Gender Transitioning and Beyond
Seth Jamison Rainess

Letters for My Brothers:
Transitional Wisdom in Retrospect (3rd edition)
Edited by Megan Rohrer and Zander Keig

Queer Rock Love

A Family Memoir

Paige Schilt

Oakland, CA

First published 2015 by Transgress Press

All rights reserved. No part of this book may be reprinted or reproduced or utilized in any form, or by electronic, mechanical, or any other means, now known or hereafter invented, including photocopying and recording, or in any information storage or retrieval system, without expressed written permission from the publisher.

Library of Congress Cataloguing in Publication Data

Queer Rock Love: A Family Memoir

Copyright © 2015 Paige Schilt

ISBN 13: 9780986084430
ISBN: 0986084433

Cover art by Rachael Shannon
Library of Congress Control Number: 2015911332
Transgress Press, Oakland, California

This is a nonfiction memoir. Events and conversations are described as I remember them or as they were told to me by people who lived them. Some names and identifying details have been changed to preserve the privacy of individuals. Any medical information contained within should be understood as the opinion of an English major whose only college science course was called "Physics for Poets."

The author gratefully acknowledges *Brain, Child* magazine, where portions of "Think Pink," "Breast Is Best" and "Boygirls and Girlboys" were first published.

The author gratefully acknowledges permission to reprint lyrics from "The Origin of Love" by Stephen Trask. Copyright ©1999 EMI April Music, Inc./so do my songs. Reprinted courtesy of Stephen Trask.

This book is dedicated to Katy and Waylon
for allowing me to share their stories.

Table of Contents

Think Pink

KATY'S MOTHER, DONNA KOONCE, wanted a baby girl.

The year was 1962. Donna and her husband Big Phil, a small-town Texas football coach, had two strapping young sons. But Donna yearned for a soul mate, a confidante, a fashion plate. In a word, she wanted a daughter.

This was before the advent of routine prenatal ultrasounds, but Donna was undaunted. A hardy optimist with a penchant for bullet bras and blond wiglets, Donna put her faith in positive thinking. She taped a picture of a baby girl to the Frigidaire. She tied pink ribbons to lampshades and chairs, where she could see them as she dusted the end tables and vacuumed the dining room.

In order to enlist the help of the community, Donna threw a "Think Pink" shower. Her friends served pink cake and adorned Donna with a corsage of pink carnations. They brought pink presents. Delicate dresses with tiny petticoats were tucked away in the nursery, which was (of course) pink.

When her due date finally arrived, Donna had a bad case of pneumonia. She arrived in the delivery room heavily drugged. The family doctor, an unassuming sadist named Grundy Cooper, knew how badly Donna wanted a girl. "Oh, *he* looks real good, Donna," Grundy teased from behind the modesty curtain that bisected her upper and lower halves.

"Shut up, Grundy, she is *not* a boy," Donna growled.

After the final push, Donna shouted, "Let me see her genitals! Let me see her genitals!" Grundy took his sweet time, holding the baby upside down, delivering the breath-inducing spank, and finally placing the tiny body on the scale so Donna could see. When the fluorescent lights of the delivery room reflected off the shiny steel cradle of the scale, Donna's drug- and hormone-addled eyes noted two things: a vulva and a hazy white halo.

"She's an angel, Phillip," she said to her husband, who had been hastily summoned from the waiting room. "She's an angel."

Nine years later, in 1971, my own parents were speeding over a bridge in their purple Volkswagen Beetle. Mom was breathing "hee, hee, hoo" as the contractions came closer together. She wanted a natural birth without drugs or modesty curtains. But she and my dad, the newly appointed Dean of Students at Indiana University Southeast, lived in the farming community of Floyds Knobs, Indiana. No local hospitals shared my mother's enthusiasm for natural childbirth, and they certainly weren't going to allow a father in the delivery room. So when mom's water broke, my parents set off across the Ohio River toward the nearest city: Louisville, Kentucky.

By the time the VW pulled up at St. Anthony Hospital, Mom was too far along to sit in a wheelchair, and she waddled into the delivery room on her own. Nuns rushed my dad into sterile gloves and a gown so that he could fulfill his duties as labor coach. He entered the delivery room just in time to see my pointy little chin emerge. "Well," said the doctor, glancing at dad's prominent features, which were presently the same pale green as the hospital walls, "she's definitely yours."

My parents' milieu of Lamaze exercises and hippie cars was worlds away from Donna Koonce's East Texas, but my mom and dad had at least one thing in common with Donna: a determination to shape their child's gender identity and expression. While Katy's mother dreamed of birthing a tiny beauty queen, my parents aspired to raise the next Gloria Steinem.

Instead of frilly dresses, my parents gave me pantsuits and a pink plaster plaque that said "Girls Can Do Anything!" They bade me good-night with the affirmation, "You can grow up to be the First Woman President." And they bought me the Sunshine Family dolls as antidote to the bimboesque influence of Barbie.

The Sunshine Family lived in a cardboard craft store, complete with spinning wheel and pottery kiln. Sunshine Mama (whose name was "Steffie") wore a calico maxi-dress, and her bare feet were realistically flat. But Steffie's half-inch waist and candy floss hair were pure Mattel fantasy. In my imaginative play, her husband, Steve, worked the cash register, while she pricked her finger on the spinning wheel. Despite Steffie's hippie accessories, her liberation was circumscribed by marriage and motherhood.

My mom and Steffie had a lot in common. Like Steffie, Mom excelled at the old-fashioned domestic arts—not because of some hippy-dippy fad, but because she had been raised Mormon. As a young girl, she had been taught to sew clothes, grow vegetables, and put up canned goods for the second coming of Christ. At eighteen, she escaped her rather stifling home life by enrolling at Arizona State University. She moved into the dorms, majored in English, and wrote a scandalous senior paper on D.H. Lawrence. A few months before graduation, she met my Catholic father. Despite her extended family's belief that she would wind up in the fiery pit of hell, she converted to Catholicism and married him before the ink was dry on her diploma.

After the wedding, Mom traded her bouffant hairdo for a fashionable shag. She wore bell-bottoms and handmade halter tops. She attended feminist consciousness-raising groups and brought home mimeographed handouts about the ERA. But she changed into a square-looking polyester dress whenever Dad needed her to perform the role of Dean's Wife, setting out trays of food at endless faculty parties and playing a dutiful second fiddle to his career success.

Thus, although *Free to Be You and Me* was in heavy rotation on my plastic ladybug record player, I grew up convinced that marriage or the convent were my only possible destinies. By the time I was eight, I had already concluded that I was too brunette and substantial to inspire romance. I regret to say that I did not indulge in proto-lesbian fantasies about convent life, but rather viewed the nun's habit as a badge of failure, a kind of scarlet V for unwanted virginity. Laura Ingalls Wilder's *Little House on the Prairie* series consoled me with the thought that a strong work ethic might make me worthy to be some man's wife. My solitary twin bed was the site of vivid fantasies about scrubbing my future husband's shirts on a tin washboard.

Early in our relationship, Katy brought over a tape of her family's home movies and a joint. She wasn't normally a pot smoker, but I think she guessed that my feminist consciousness was going to need expanding if we were to swap childhood stories in the way that new lovers do. She'd dated enough Women's Studies majors to guess that "the cultural construction of gender" would be my mantra, the magic words that were supposed to save me from the depressing determinism of biology as destiny and the one-size-fits-all essentialism of universal sisterhood.

Savvy as she was, she could hardly have anticipated the intensity of my views. I leaned fervently, incontrovertibly toward the nurture side of the nature vs. nurture debate. If anyone spoke to me of gender as something innate or remotely natural, I did the intellectual equivalent of covering my ears and shouting, "La, la, la, I can't hear you!"

In my heart, I believed that acknowledging a biological component to gender was a slippery slope that would land me right back in front of that washboard, scrubbing some man's collars.

Now, in reel after reel, I discovered Katy at 2, 3, and 4—already miraculously masculine, already chaffing like a football player in frilly dresses, already looking dejected when she unwrapped yet another doll from underneath the Christmas tree.

Suddenly, the whole notion of nature *vs.* nurture ceased to make sense. Her pintsize Texan masculinity was culturally pitch-perfect—and a total violation of the prevailing gender system. It was incongruent with anatomy—and undeniably physical, emanating from every muscle and gesture.

The highlight of the home movie footage was the year when Katy appeared next to the Christmas tree in full Davy Crockett costume. Freed from the confines of fussy dresses, she sprawled on the floor next to a long, rectangular package. A second later, the wrapping paper was off, and she was jumping up and down, triumphantly brandishing a new BB gun.

Having grown up with the peaceful Sunshine Family, I was hardly accustomed to celebrating childhood gun ownership...and yet, I found myself strangely un-horrified. There was something undeniably liberating in her joy, something that forced me to reach beyond my usual knee-jerk reactions. Maybe it was the pot. Or maybe I was falling in love.

"Dude," I said, "this is blowing my mind."

Part I

CHAPTER 1

Man-Chest

THE FIRST TIME I ever saw Katy, she was wearing a full beard and a prosthetic man-chest with perfectly molded pecs and sculpted abs. It was 1999 in Austin, Texas, and she was playing bass for Raunchy Reckless and the Amazons, a Xena-inspired art band whose motto, "Keep the dream alive," was literalized in outrageous costumes that transformed private fantasies into fabulous public realities. Katy's character was called "Koonce the Vulgar Viking," and she sang a catchy song about her masculine physique:

> All the girls love it,
> While the scrawny boys want it.
> Don't you wanna touch it?
> Don't you wanna touch it?
> Man-chest!

The man-chest was just a piece of molded rubber, the kind of thing you might buy as a gag at Halloween, but it looked comfortable—even sexy—on Koonce the Viking. I *did* want to touch it, but I was standing in the back of the darkened room, selling t-shirts to support Girlday, a riot grrrl-inspired feminist conference that I had co-founded with my sister and some friends. I hadn't come out yet, and the crowded bar—packed with sweaty, dancing, sexy queers—filled me with longing and despair.

A year later, I was getting ready to go on stage before an audience of sweaty, dancing, sexy queers. In a desperate attempt to shed my straight-girl reputation and find a girlfriend, I had volunteered to be a go-go girl at Hip-Hop 4 Laydeez, a semi-regular roving dance party that could transform even the most mundane dive into a cruise-y, pulsating dyke bar.

The location for the evening was Gaby and Mo's, an appliance-repair-shop-turned-coffeehouse that served as Austin's main lesbian social space. Behind a triptych of plate-glass windows, the enterprising owners had erected a tiny stage. Where once dusty toaster ovens had been stacked on top of boxy televisions, now slam poets beseeched unwary undergrads and all-girl country bands serenaded awkward correspondents from the women-seeking-women section of the personals ads.

Tonight, all the chairs and tables had been pushed to the back of the room and the cafe's red and pink walls had been festooned with streamers and paper hearts.

It was Valentine's Day, and I was on a mission to make out with hotties. To this end, I had traded my black-rimmed glasses for false eyelashes and a pair of rarely used contact lenses. As I clambered atop the stage in tiny hot pants and 4-inch platform heels, I realized the fatal flaw in my plan: I am not a gifted dancer. I am the kind of person who dances with brow furrowed in concentration. Furthermore, I hadn't listened to pop music since junior high. My idea of a good dance song was something that allowed you to thrash wildly, like Sleater Kinney or Sonic Youth. Now, complex beats pumped from the speakers behind me, punctuating my total lack of rhythm. Partygoers began to pour in the doors, and my face flushed as bright as the pink and red walls.

Suddenly, someone was saying my name.

"Paige? Do you want me to fix that spotlight? It's shining right in your eyes."

S/he wasn't wearing a full beard or a prosthetic man-chest, but I knew immediately that it was the Viking from Raunchy Reckless. I also knew that this person, with his or her butch chivalry, was the sexiest thing I had ever seen. And s/he knew my name! I had a crush so brutal and instantaneous that I could barely speak.

"No," I mumbled, turning my face away from the spotlight and the directness of Katy's gaze. "It's okay."

Katy shrugged and walked back to her friends. My heart skipped a beat. I had blown my chance! And now I had to dance all night with that stupid light shining in my eyes.

Later that same week, on February 18, 2000, *The Austin Chronicle* ran one of its first major stories about transgender issues. The previous year, a teenage trans woman named Lauryn Paige Fuller had been murdered. Now her killer was on trial, and the story had awakened Austin to the vulnerable plight of trans street kids.

Because we shared a name, I felt a particular connection with Lauryn Paige, and I scoured the news for details of her life. The *Chronicle* story quoted a local therapist named Katy Koonce, who spoke about the lack of social support for young trans women. I made a mental note to contact Ms. Koonce to find out whether Girlday might be able to help.

A few days after the *Chronicle* story appeared, I was driving to my first group therapy session. For months I had been trying to finish my dissertation on tropes of disempowerment in the work of liberal documentary filmmakers, and it was taking a toll on my mental health. All my life I had been the teacher's pet, sustained by the instant validation I got from producing the correct answers in class. Now my coursework was completed, and I labored alone in the tiny 3 x 5 cubicle that the University of Texas issued to dissertation writers. Lonely and full of self-doubt, I veered between manic attempts at manufactured approval and dark days when I couldn't stop crying. Finally, a therapy-savvy friend suggested group therapy. Talking about my issues in front of seven or eight total strangers? It sounded terrifying, but at least it would be a respite from my cramped cubicle. Anyway, I was desperate. Despite occasional forays into go-go dancing, I couldn't seem to shake this depression on my own.

I pulled into the parking lot 20 minutes early. I'd visited the office before, to meet with the group leader, but I still had no idea what to expect from an hour and a half of sharing with fellow therapy seekers. *What if no one speaks to me? What if no one likes me? What if they can see how lonely and depressed I am?* Not wanting to appear too eager, I wandered across the street to smoke. As I brought the lighter to my cigarette, I noticed that my hands were shaking.

Two cigarettes later, I gathered enough courage to go inside. The waiting room was empty, but the door to the inner office was open and half a dozen men and women were already seated in a crowded circle of couches and chairs. I took a spot close to the door. In the unforgiving light of self-consciousness, my prospective peers looked like they had been photographed by Diane Arbus. I began to have serious doubts about this whole group thing. What was I doing with all these warped and broken-looking people?

Just as I was about to make a run for it, a majestic figure came barreling down the hall and through the office door. Head tilted, long hair falling forward like a shield—it was the Viking. And s/he pointed straight at me.

"I know you," Katy said, and plopped into the chair next to mine.

Group therapy is a strange place to start a relationship.

Before we ever spent a moment alone together, Katy knew that I was a depression-prone approval-seeker with an addiction to vintage clothes. She also knew that I was divorced, that I was ambivalent about my academic career, and that I tended to smile and joke when I was hurt or angry.

I knew that Katy was a former drug addict with hepatitis C. I knew she had a girlfriend, and that their relationship was strained by Katy's many health problems. I knew that Katy's anger could command a room, but her vulnerability could take my breath away.

We bonded over body issues. I had grown up in a family of compulsive dieters. My mom drifted from fad to fad, cooking cauldrons of cabbage soup and later filling our cupboards with cardboard-tasting NutriSystems snacks. In the early years of the low-fat diet craze, my dad subsisted solely on grapes and bagels. Thanks to a well-timed growth spurt, I had escaped the full force of my parents' obsession with weight loss, but I saw them interrogate my younger sister's every mouthful, until she always felt too big, no matter how much weight she lost.

Similarly, in Katy's family, "lose some weight" was the parental response to everything from hangnail to heartache. As an adult, Katy wore oversized men's shirts with outlandish patterns. They were calculated to distract the eye and disguise her body. I longed to run my hands down her back, to explore whether she was wearing a chest binder or an undershirt or nothing at all.

In one of our earliest sessions, Katy was agonizing because she had been misquoted in the *Austin Chronicle* story on Lauryn Paige. Suddenly, it dawned on me: Katy from group = Koonce the Vulgar Viking = that smart therapist from the newspaper. But while I was impressed, Katy was mortified, because the reporter had bungled the distinction between sex and gender and sexuality.

To be fair, it was an era with a pretty steep learning curve. New language and new identities were proliferating. Although she used a feminine name and feminine pronouns, Katy also ran a support group for transgender men. I guessed that she was moving toward transition, but that her own identity hadn't quite caught up to the available options.

As a scholar, I was struggling to keep up as well. In college, I had written a thesis about gender and performance—which gave me license to explore everything from the butch-femme performance art duo Split Britches to the campy "dyke daddies" issue of *On Our Backs*. I told myself that all of this information gathering was strictly for research purposes, but in private moments my mind tended to linger on certain pieces of "data" (like the moment in *Angry Women* when Annie Sprinkle talks about having sex with her trans boyfriend.)

Now, six years later, I was finishing a dissertation chapter on the documentary *Paris Is Burning*. Initially, most of the critical responses had framed the film as a representation of a black gay subculture, but now there was a growing sophistication about the differences between drag queens and transsexuals and the specificity of trans experiences. As a lowly graduate student, I puzzled over these cultural shifts—all the while assuring myself that my interest in trans subcultures was merely academic.

Apparently Katy wasn't the only one whose identity hadn't caught up to the available options.

Our therapist, Jeff, was a mild-mannered redhead with a shitload of unacknowledged aggression. In keeping with the therapeutic mantra that "everything is grist for the mill," Jeff encouraged Katy and me to share our growing infatuation, which was mortifying (because it was so public) but also gratifying (because the feelings were mutual). In his breathy, singsong voice, Jeff cautioned that group crushes were common but fleeting phantasms of projection. As if to prove his point, he asked Katy to describe her perfect partner. "I know one thing," she said, sweeping back her dark hair. "I want to be parents together."

In an instant, I was jolted from my cocoon of infatuation. I had never wanted to be a parent. In fact, I had married my former husband with the explicit understanding that we would never breed. In my twenties, when friends spoke about the ticking of biological clocks, I was relieved not to have alarms buzzing in my ovaries. After all, I was an aspiring academic, and I saw how dismissively faculty and students treated women who got pregnant before tenure.

Then, when I was 27, I had a whirlwind affair with a brilliant and mercurial poet. He swept me off my feet, I left my marriage, and we spent the next two years making each other's lives miserable. We broke up and got back together more times than I could count, and it was during one of our cathartic reunions in his little poet's cottage that I ended up getting pregnant.

I was a couple years away from finishing school, with no particularly lucrative source of income, and a doomed relationship. Deep in my heart, I suspected that I was a lesbian, but I kept waiting for someone in a position of authority to give me a badge and welcome me to the club. In the absence of any resounding cultural encouragement for being queer, I hovered at the edges of my own life. On the night I got pregnant, I was watching myself from the ceiling, like a mildly interested but not too invested spectator—one who apparently didn't care to remind herself that she'd stopped taking her birth control pills a few weeks earlier.

Pregnancy brought me plummeting back to my body. Before I even missed my period, I *knew*. And this intuition, while terrifying, was not altogether unpleasant.

I'd always assumed that I'd know exactly what to do if I got pregnant, but now I found myself pulled in all directions. My ex was leaving me tearful late-night messages, begging me not to "kill our baby." These filled me with rage and stoked my fears about saddling a child with a manipulative and dysfunctional dad. My family was much better; they told me that they'd support me no matter what. But, in a clan that valued career success above almost everything else, it was no real mystery what they thought I should do. Having a baby would derail my dissertation and delay graduation. It would be awkward in job interviews and maybe even keep me from finding the holy grail: a tenure-track job.

I wanted to go with my gut, but my gut flinched at the thought of telling my professors and fellow grad students that I was going to have a baby. I was afraid of looking like a fuck-up. I was afraid of disappointing people. I was afraid I'd find myself even further away from the queer community that I craved.

In the end, I had an abortion. Like most decisions motivated by fear, it made me feel small and sad. Even after I severed ties with the poet, even when I finally went on a date with a woman, I still felt like I was living a life with the smallest possible footprint, afraid to do anything that would displease my friends and family. Some days I actually felt like I was disappearing. Which is how I ended up in group therapy. Which is why, when Katy sat across from me in the group and said that she imagined herself and her future partner "walking down Congress Avenue on Sunday mornings, pushing our baby stroller and waving to the dykes at Jo's Coffee," I didn't run screaming in the opposite direction.

As strange as it sounds, this fragmentary image soothed my fears. I'm not saying that I started knitting baby booties. But, under the influence of Katy's fantasy, I stopped thinking of motherhood as a retreat from being a lez. In a sense, I realized, becoming a parent might make me even more visibly queer.

We saw each other once a week for an hour and a half, in a room full of other people. Six months later, I took a job in Pennsylvania and said goodbye to the group. The night before my moving van arrived, Katy and I took a picnic to the top of Mount Bonnell—ostensibly because I wanted to see the lights of the city one last time but really because I wanted to have her all to myself.

We loitered long after the park had closed. Lying next to her on a rocky cliff, I could feel the heat of the day radiating up from the limestone. Words spilled out of us, unleashing invisible vectors of energy that bounced back and forth in the narrow space between our arms. My whole body buzzed with anticipation and restraint.

The next day, I packed up my last few boxes and headed north. Despite the fact that I was moving 1,500 miles away, despite the fact that we had never even kissed, I felt strangely confident that we would be together.

CHAPTER 2

Put a Ring on It

KATY CLAIMS THAT IT happened like this:

We were in my car, heading north. She was behind the wheel. "If we were straight," she said, turning to the passenger side, "I'd take you to Atlantic City and marry you right now."

And then, purportedly, I said, "For all this talk of marriage, I don't see a ring on my finger."

There are two problems with this scenario. First, I am not a coquette. It is not my custom to speak like a latter-day lesbian Scarlet O'Hara. Second, I am not a believer. I'm the divorced child of divorced parents. I don't venerate marriage as a natural state, a keystone of civilization, or even a particularly convenient model of intimate relationship.

Still, "I don't see a ring on my finger" are the words that, according to the only other extant witness, I am supposed to have uttered on September 10, 2000.

This was our second date. I had recently relocated from Austin to rural Pennsylvania. As a newly minted English Ph.D., I was eager to take advantage of a three-year visiting professor gig at a small liberal arts college just west of the Allegheny River. Never mind that my new home was two hours from the nearest airport. Or that the local lesbians lived like maiden aunts. Or that the weather forecast called for snow from October to May. All the better, I told myself; I'll hole up by the fire and write.

But I wasn't writing. I was thinking of Katy. So I invited her to visit my rural abode.

A weeklong second date is a risky proposition. Since I had left Austin, we'd thrown caution to the wind, confessing our dearest hopes and desires over lengthy long-distance telephone calls. By the time Katy arrived at the airport, we were already building a future on the flimsy foundation of flirtatious conversation. But we hadn't even kissed yet. If our physical chemistry didn't match our conversational chemistry, we would have to suffer a long and awkward seven days.

After our first kiss (in the baggage claim area), we did considerably less talking.

Five days later, we came up for air. Our time together was almost over, and I wanted to find something special to mark the end of our epic date.

A colleague told me about Lily Dale, New York, a Victorian-era village populated by psychics. I knew that my new love had an affinity for the supernatural, and I thought it would make an amusing day trip.

Founded in 1879, Lily Dale quaintly bills itself as the largest spiritualist community in the world—as if municipalities worldwide are vying to be the capitol of a nineteenth century fad. In Lily Dale's heyday, spirits knocked on tables and powerful mediums oozed ectoplasmic goo. These days, so-called "physical manifestations" are frowned upon. But Lily Dale is still home to 90 registered mediums, who commune with the dead in both private consultations and regularly scheduled public meetings.

It's a strange place for a romantic getaway. Most pilgrims are grieving. They come in search of answers about the death of a child or lover. They want to know where the treasure is hidden or whether their dearly beloved is resting peacefully on the other side.

Katy and I arrived just after the regular season, which lasts from June to August. The weather had turned wet and windy, and mud puddles clotted the narrow streets. Standing water glistened from bright green Astroturf on the ramshackle porches of aging Victorian cottages. It looked like several generations of American optimism had collided and fallen into benign disrepair.

Holding hands, Katy and I followed the path to a pet cemetery in a stand of ancient trees. Under their lush green canopy, Katy told me about the deaths of her dogs, Face and General Lee. She told me about her best friend Jane Ellen, who had promised to visit in dreams after she died. Sitting on a stump in the shade of the forest, Katy told me about her crystal meth days, when she could walk into a library or a metaphysical bookstore and literally hear books calling her name.

Normally, this kind of talk caused me to roll my eyes.

As a teenager, I had witnessed my mother's New Age awakening, when she bought a condo in Santa Fe and consulted a psychic to help her find husband number three. Surrounded by tanned white people with positive vibrations, I had resisted with the only weapons I knew—sunscreen and a bad attitude. As soon as I could, I fled to college in the gothic mists of the Pacific Northwest. I vowed that folk art angels would never adorn my home.

Rather than putting me off, Katy's mysticism made me want to get closer. Her drug-induced visions of talking books had a dark, malevolent edge that was missing from the usual New Age blather. The darkness allowed me to relax my constant vigilance and adopt a guardedly curious posture toward things that I habitually disavowed.

It helped that she had all the trappings of a Romantic hero: long, dark hair, a prominent brow, and a death sentence. When she quit drugs a decade earlier, Katy had been diagnosed with hepatitis C. The future looked like cirrhosis or cancer. Then, a few years later, a new generation of antiviral drugs brought hope for people with hepatitis C. Katy had weathered their punishing regimen—only to find that her particular strain of the virus did not respond. Now she spoke matter-of-factly about her early expiration date.

"When I'm 65, I'll start drinking again," she said. "We can go on one of those Delbert McClinton blues cruises and booze it up until my liver gives out."

I nodded my head. I had no idea who Delbert McClinton was. In her company, I felt unmarked by loss and experience. Being with her was like visiting another planet. It was like fucking an alien.

I told her about my recently deceased cat, for whom I had built a small (secular) shrine. I told her about my exes, which were the closest things I had to ghosts.

Despite all the stereotypes of lesbian merging, I had no intention of actually changing my mind about New Age spirituality. However, because I was drunk on infatuation, and because I wanted to continue having exciting alien sex, I didn't voice my usual opinions on mediums (quacks), the afterlife (unlikely), or monogamous marriage (extremely unlikely).

We kissed in the dappled light under the trees. An old man in overalls wandered past the headstones of long-dead pets. I was wearing a blue vintage dress and spiky hair. Katy was wearing combat boots and a black bowling shirt with the name "Dick" emblazoned on the pocket. I wondered, when the old man looked at us, did he see a man and a woman? Or two dykes defiling the woods?

We emerged from the forest and into the circle of Victorian houses where mediums entertain spiritual seekers. My ambivalence was like a powerful alternating current, propelling us up the stairs of each house and then repelling us back down into the street. Each time we found a medium at home, Katy looked at me, trying to sense whether *this* was the one. Each time, I shook my head no.

In truth, I did not want to get a reading because I was afraid that Katy would see my disbelief. I did not want to pretend to believe, but I didn't want her to think I was incapable of believing, either. It was confusing. The air was full of other people's hope and grief and yearning. They mixed with my own swirling feelings and manifested as a lump in the back of my throat.

I do not know if Katy sensed my ambivalence. Having grown up in a culture of ruthless affirmation, I had learned to hide mixed feelings. But, as a dissenter, I had also learned to trust my instincts. And now my instincts were guiding me to the Crystal Cove Gift Shop.

In the car, when the subject of weddings had arisen, Katy had predicted that a place like Lily Dale would surely have a crystal shop with rings. Now that we had passed up all of the potential mediums, she suggested that we seek it out.

Inside the Crystal Cove, I felt like the planchette on a Ouija board. I glided to the jewelry case. Scanning the rows of quartz and hematite, my eyes lit on a silver diamante figure eight, an ersatz antique infinity symbol.

"Can I try that one?" I asked the heavily bejeweled white woman behind the counter. I thought, *I can't believe I'm doing this.* Then I thought, *I want it.*

While the saleswoman was busy below the counter, I glanced at Katy to see if I was overstepping the bounds. She looked happy and excited. She told me that the ring was perfect for me. I wanted something of hers to keep. (Later, before she went back to Texas, I would steal her shirt and keep it under my pillow, where I could press it to my face at night and breathe her in.)

If the ring fits, that will be a sign.

It fit.

I kept looking at Katy. *Are we really doing this?* She was selecting a ring for herself, a chunky Celtic design that looked at home on her big hand.

We paid for each other's souvenirs. Back outside, we sat on a wrought-iron bench bedecked with cherubs. We hadn't spoken about what, exactly, we were up to. Now two small, white cardboard jewelry boxes were sitting between us. Katy looked nervous. I closed my eyes and searched for words and ritual that would consecrate the moment without overwhelming it.

"I love you," I said.

"I love you," she replied. Tears streamed down both of our faces. I was crying because I was vulnerable and because it was okay. The lump in my throat was fading away. I felt for the rings and removed hers from the box.

"With this ring, I thee wed," I said, quickly. I slipped the ring on her finger and smiled.

"With this ring, I thee wed," she echoed. She slipped the ring on my finger.

I did not believe in mediums, but I was beginning to believe in the future.

CHAPTER 3

The Universe Speaks

THE UNIVERSE WAS SPEAKING. It was speaking to Katy's friend, Jim Cramer, whose initials just happened to be J.C.

I was living in Pennsylvania, trying to make it through the long northern winter. Katy was down in Austin, finishing her clinical internship at a low-cost community counseling center. During our nightly phone conversations, she told me stories about a brilliant, charismatic coworker named Jim. At Jim's urging, Katy had joined a psychoanalytic study group, and together they were becoming the *enfants terribles* of the counseling center, quoting theory in staff meetings and demanding that harried supervisors with armloads of paperwork entertain nebulous concepts like *projective identification* and *extractive introjection*.

Jim had recently divorced and sold his marital home in South Austin. He wanted to stay in the 78704, a part of town famous for its hodgepodge of hippy, Mexican, and musical cultures, but old South Austin was changing. Little shotgun houses with musty couches on front porches were giving way to stuccoed condos with rectangles of manicured lawn. Prices were becoming pretty steep for a single social worker.

Every day, Jim combed the neighborhood with his fat yellow lab, Goldie Hawn, looking for a house he could afford. The one that eventually caught his eye had originally been a two-bedroom cottage, but the current owner had built a second, identical cottage on the second story. When a sign appeared in the front yard, "For Sale—Duplex," it was the answer to Jim's prayers. He couldn't afford to buy a house in South Austin on his own. But he could afford to buy half a house.

The next morning in study group, Jim was preoccupied with finding a partner in real estate. When his eyes landed on Katy, his professional ally and co-conspirator, it seemed like a Sign: they were meant to buy a house together. And, because Katy and I had decided that we were married, that meant that I was meant to buy a house with Jim too.

That night on the phone, Katy told me that she and Jim were going to look at a house in South Austin. "He says it just has this remarkable energy." I rolled my eyes in the privacy of my Pennsylvania apartment, and Katy continued unaware. "He thinks we ought to buy it together. It's a duplex, so we could live in the top and he could live in the bottom."

"Hmm…" I said. In my heart I had decided to move back to Austin, but I hadn't given much thought to where we would live. I was filled with dread at the prospect of telling everyone—my department chair, my mentors, and especially my parents—that I was quitting my job. Through six grueling years of grad school, life had seemed linear. If all went well, I would land a tenure track position and move up the ladder at regularly scheduled intervals. Now I felt like I was sailing over the edge of the known universe in a barrel. I wasn't entirely sure if I would survive the journey. What did I care for the details of how we might live when (and if) I arrived?

A few nights later, Katy brought it up again. "You're going to love it," she said. "There's something about it…it's just got the greatest energy." I tried to remain noncommittal, but suddenly Katy was talking mortgage lenders and down payments.

"But," I objected, "I haven't even met Jim! How can I buy a house with someone I've never met?"

My feeble sandbags were no match for the tidal wave of Katy's enthusiasm. "You're going to love him too," she assured me. "He's super smart, and he reads Lacan! I think you guys actually have a lot in common."

Despite my trepidations about the house, I was looking forward to spending winter break in Austin with Katy. Two weeks would be the longest we'd ever been together in the same space, a test of our domestic compatibility. The day after I arrived, Katy whisked me off to see our potential new home.

From the street, it was a little underwhelming. The front porch was a lopsided slab of concrete, and the second story addition had been finished with canary yellow siding, but the agent ushered us around to the huge backyard, which was big and deep and dominated by a majestic, many-branched ash tree.

The current tenants habitually used the back entrance, because both were running home businesses in violation of the neighborhood zoning laws. The ground floor was occupied by a bearded New Age guy who directed a mysterious organization with the acronym "E.A.T." (The "E" was for eternal, but the rest of the initials escape me now.) It might sound like an organization named "eat" would distribute food, but I think he was mostly concerned with cleansing the remains of food from his clients' colons. The front bedroom served as a waiting room, and the back room hosted a colonic hydrotherapy machine. Above the shiny apparatus, a sign proclaimed the life-giving properties of "the angel of water."

The upper apartment was occupied by a holistic aesthetician who gave facials in the front room and lived in the back bedroom, but you'd never guess that anyone did anything as messy or unpredictable as eating or sleeping there. As we crossed the threshold, the agent asked us to remove our shoes and place them in a rack by the door. Piñon incense wafted through the air. With the exception of a few pieces of rustic folk art, the walls were pristine white, and the entire suite was spotless. There were tiny mirrors above the doors, talismans to deflect evil spirits.

An hour after we saw the house, I was sitting in a dark Mexican restaurant across from a short, wiry white man with thinning hair. "Well?" Jim asked eagerly, "What did you think? Isn't it magical?"

I hesitated. The house *did* seem magical—in part because it was about 100 times cleaner than any of the rent houses and apartments I'd occupied in my adult life. The upstairs, where Katy and I would live, was practically new, with modern conveniences like a dishwasher and a disposal and windows that weren't painted shut. I couldn't put my finger on any one thing that was wrong with the house—except for the fact that Katy and I had never lived together for longer than a few days at a time and it was totally insane to think about buying a house so soon.

Jim's enthusiasm was not about to be squelched by my ambivalence. He waxed poetic about the epic parties we could throw in our big backyard. "There's a perfect place to put a hot tub, and those two trees against the fence line, they're just the right distance for a hammock. The garage apartment isn't finished out yet, but that's great because it means we can do whatever we want with it. Katy and I could use it for therapy offices or we could turn it into a live music venue and have shows back there."

I raised an eyebrow at Katy. The space was special, sure, but it would take a miracle to transform a 700-square-foot garage apartment into a live music venue. "I think Paige has some ideas about how to use the space," Katy said helpfully. I could tell she was desperate to help me find a foothold in the conversation.

"I'm going to need an office too," I said flatly. It was my one stipulation about our future home. I had no idea what kind of work I'd be able to find back in Austin, but I knew that I needed a room of my own.

"Well, sure," Jim countered without skipping a beat, "that's why your part of the house has two bedrooms. One of those rooms can be your office."

I was shocked that my needs could be so summarily dispatched. I did not like this man with a plan for me and my space. If you'd asked me right that second if I wanted to buy a house with him, I would have said *no way.*

After lunch, Katy and I dropped by the Montgomery Ward going-out-of-business sale. I had insisted that we buy a new frame for Katy's ancient king-sized bed, which was really a king mattress atop two twin box springs. Following a night of passion, the center part would sag and we'd end up squished against each other like the filling in a fold-over sandwich. The new frame was to be our first joint purchase.

By the time we arrived at the dilapidated strip mall, Montgomery's carcass was nearly picked clean. Lucky for us, there was still one last king-sized bed frame in the stock room. We waited in a line of dedicated bargain seekers, forked over $50, took a number, and headed out to the loading dock to wait.

In the parking lot, we joined a crowd of people who looked to have been waiting a long time. There was no real place to sit, so we hunkered down on the sidewalk. It was a hot, humid Texas December day, and my three-quarter-sleeve vintage cashmere sweater was already beginning to smell like sweat and mothballs.

"Well," Katy asked, "what did you think?"

"About what?" I wondered, stalling for time. My eyes darted to the people leaving the front of the store. They were dragging fixtures—display cases and chrome dress racks—through the swinging glass doors. A sign in the front window said EVERYTHING MUST GO.

"About Jim," Katy insisted, reeling me back in.

"Well...he's kind of intense. He talked a lot."

"He was nervous," she explained. "He's not always like that."

The sun was melting my makeup. I felt exposed.

"He seems very smart," I said, smiling brightly.

People always talked about my smile. "You look so happy all the time," they said. It wasn't until I squirmed in the spotlight of group therapy that my smile had become a problem, nay a pathology. "You're smiling again," Jeff would say, with a tsk-tsk in his voice. "What are you really feeling?"

Often I was feeling anything but cheerful. The smile tended to shine most brilliantly when I was feeling angry or scared or any of the other feelings that had been deemed unseemly in my family. Worse yet, the smile crept out without my conscious knowledge. Before I started group therapy, I hadn't realized that I smiled like a maniac through the most painful encounters. Now it made me think of a song I'd learned in

Brownies: "I've got something in my pocket, it belongs across my face." Only, in my case, the smile was like a zombie limb that crawled out of my pocket with a mind of its own.

Sitting in the parking lot of the Montgomery Ward, I cursed Jeff for spoiling a perfectly good defense. I couldn't tell if Katy knew that I was smiling *that* smile, but somehow her steadfast gaze pierced through the shell and into the turmoil below. I started to cry.

"What's wrong?" Katy asked, gathering me to her chest. A woman in Bermuda shorts and an oversized t-shirt looked at us and shook her head. Bored kids were running all around us, and I desperately wanted to pull it together before I attracted their attention. But if I stopped crying, that would require me to give an account of myself and my distress, and I wasn't sure what was causing the tears. Was it the looming dread over quitting my job? Was it Jim's personality, which seemed so big that I couldn't imagine what space would be left in our shared house? Or was the prospect of buying real estate suddenly making everything—the whole whirlwind love affair—too real?

"I'm fine," I said, wiping my tears and taking a deep breath. "I'm just feeling a little overwhelmed."

Later that night, we lay in the newly buttressed king-size bed and ate fudge that Katy had made from Jet-Puffed Marshmallow Cream. It was unabashedly lowbrow—like green bean casserole made from Campbell's soup, the kind of thing my family would never deign to eat—yet it was undeniably delicious. We were watching reruns of VH1 Behind the Music, chortling at the hackneyed narration, and all the while my hand kept creeping back to the fudge tin. After each piece, I licked my fingers, resolving not to take another bite, but it was too good to resist for long.

When the tin was nearly empty, I probed for the pang of guilt that usually accompanied any kind of indulgence or unproductive time. Clearly we were wasting the evening, clearly we were eating "too much" fudge, but Katy wasn't going to lament with me. She didn't have guilty pleasures. She liked what she liked—whether it was bad TV or marshmallow cream—and she didn't apologize. I wanted to be like that, to do what I liked and let the fudge crumbs fall where they may.

Normally I would have reached for a stack of papers to grade or an article I needed to read—some penance to try to justify the sorry space I occupied on the planet. Instead, I settled further into the voluminous bed. Since Katy and I had gotten together, the whole academic career trajectory—writing articles, searching for a tenure-track job, spending six more years jumping through tenure hoops—seemed surprisingly optional. I had spent my whole life learning the skills I needed to walk that path: discernment, self-discipline, and conciliation. I had scurried along, full of guilt and anxiety, smiling like a maniac and terrified of making mistakes. It was a revelation to step off the wheel, to see the whole thing from another vantage point.

I realized, to my surprise, that I was more afraid of losing Katy than I was of making a mistake. No matter how stupid it might be to quit my job, no matter how risky buying a house with a stranger, I felt certain about Katy and all that she had to teach me. *WWKD?* I wondered. *What would Katy do?*

I pictured myself back in the restaurant with Jim. In my mind's eye, I sat up straight and assumed my full height. *I'm not going to be scared of you, little man. You can't tell me what to do or where to put my office.* It almost seemed laughable that I had been so frightened earlier.

"Babe," I said at the commercial break, "Let's do it! Let's make an offer on the house."

"Really?" Katy's face lit up with pleasure and surprise. "Are you sure? Jim's not too much for you?"

"No, he's not too much. And the house has really good energy."

CHAPTER 4

Meet the Parents

IN 1981, WHEN KATY came home for Christmas with a "friend," her mother "accidentally" discovered their love letters in the girlfriend's purse. Donna called the girls to the living room, where she presided over the house from a green velour recliner. Trembling, Katy and her girlfriend awaited judgment on the couch. Mom stared the girlfriend down.

"Do you love her?" she asked, finally.

"Yes," said the young woman, sneaking a glance at Katy, "I do."

"Well, good," Donna answered, taking a drag on her cigarette. "You better."

Katy told me this story as we sped down highway 71 in her bronze pick-up truck. We were headed to Lake Jackson, Texas, to meet the family, and I was full of questions. The early 1980s were the era of panic over the new "gay cancer." Only a few years earlier, Anita Bryant and her minions had campaigned to remove anyone who supported gay rights from positions in California public schools. Katy's dad was a high school football coach—a position of considerable visibility and social standing in a small Texas town. So how did her mother, a Southern belle from the piney woods of East Texas, come to unquestioning acceptance and support for her butch lesbian daughter?

Katy told me her mother was hard to explain. When Donna went to the bank to make a deposit, she refused to deal with anyone below a senior vice president. If she made reservations for a restaurant, she asked to speak with the manager before dropping her own name: "This is Donna Koonce, do you have a good table for me tonight?" If Donna sent you to the Kroger for a cut of meat, she'd remind you to "tell 'em you're a Koonce."

If a Koonce was gay, then, by Donna's logic, gay was good.

My own coming out story could not have been more different. In the fall of 1992, I accompanied my dad on a work trip to Washington, D.C. At the time, Dad was the chancellor of the University of Houston, and he was in the nation's capital to meet with foundations and wealthy donors. I was attending college in Seattle, but I jumped at the chance to tag along. I had something important to discuss.

On the last night of our stay, we were sitting in a dark, cozy corner of my dad's favorite D.C. restaurant. A waiter poured round globes of red wine, which I was only barely old enough to drink in public. Dad took a sip, gave an appreciative nod, and then perused the menu for a moment. "I'm interested in the sea bass. Shall we do our usual?" The usual meant ordering two entrées, plus a bunch of appetizers and sides, and then sharing everything between us.

"Dad, I'm a vegetarian now."

"Oh, right. I guess I'll have to eat the sea bass all by myself." He grinned a slightly sarcastic smile.

Setting his menu aside, Dad turned the warm spotlight of his conversational attention on me. He had an extraordinary ability to draw people out, especially young people. Like a combination therapist and guidance counselor, he was perfectly willing to have a long, patient conversation about a twenty-one-year-old's current interests and future plans. It was one of the things that made him such a charismatic and successful educator.

"What makes you so excited about Bill Clinton?" Dad asked. "For a while you were behind—what was his name? Harkin?" When it came to politics, Dad affected a vague, nonpartisan civic-mindedness that allowed him to avoid conflicts with wealthy alums and university regents.

"I think Clinton really cares about equality," I said. Clinton had given a speech near my university that fall—a speech in which he actually said the word "gay." I was too young to be cynical about promises made on the campaign trail. "I think..." I hesitated. "I think he cares about the rights of gay Americans."

My dad's face arranged itself into something between a frown and a cipher. He did not inquire further about this stance, but only made a noncommittal "hmmm," and raised a hand to summon the waiter.

Dad was hell on waiters. While he interrogated the poor man about various sauces and preparations—*Was the fish cooked in butter? Could he have it grilled instead of sautéed?*—I tried to summon the words I'd planned. *Was it "Dad, I'm gay?" Or "Dad, I think I might be gay?" Or "Dad, I'm attracted to women?" Oh God.* I gave my order in a daze and watched the waiter's retreat with dread.

I was desperate for an ounce of encouragement—a nod, a smile. In my best-case scenario, I had dared to hope that Dad would actually help me out. "Is there something on your mind, Sweetheart? You seem preoccupied." But no. Each time I opened my mouth to speak, I felt like an invisible force on the other side of the table was pushing the words back down my throat.

I took a big swig of wine. "So Dad," I said, hating myself for my cowardice. "What time does your flight leave tomorrow?"

I returned from the D.C. trip convinced that my dad had known what I wanted to say, but that he couldn't or wouldn't deal with it. I had another discouraging experience when I tried to talk to my boyfriend of two years. That time, I actually managed to get the words out. But as soon as I stammered that I thought I might be attracted to women, his face contorted and he started to cry. I ended up apologizing and consoling him, stroking his back while his body was wracked with sobs. "Shh-shh-shh-shh-shh. It's okay. Hey now, I'm probably not even gay."

After that, my instinct was to back away, to avoid further situations that would make me feel inarticulate and alone. I began to have convenient doubts. If I were really a lesbian, wouldn't I feel an irresistible compulsion to make my truth known? Surely my hesitation said something about me, about my so-called gayness. Maybe I was only politically gay? Maybe I was simply seduced by the lure of community, the rejection of patriarchy, the righteous anger in the face of AIDS and violence. I wanted to go to ACT UP meetings, to make out with a woman on the steps of the state capitol, to chant, "silence equals death" at scurrilous politicians. On the other hand, I really hated the way my leg hairs stood on end when I tried to grow them out. I looked terrible in a baseball cap, and I loved lipstick and dresses. Maybe I was merely bisexual—in which case, why bother to upset the apple cart if I could really get along just fine?

In the end, I decided I didn't have enough evidence to come out after all. I continued to live with my boyfriend, graduated from college, and found a part-time job as a technical librarian at an aerospace company. On the bus to work, I read *Moby Dick* and *The Scarlet Letter*—canonical works I'd missed in an undergraduate career focused on queer and feminist art. I applied to graduate school in English. When I was accepted to the University of Texas at Austin, I asked my boyfriend to marry me.

"Really?" he asked. He seemed surprised, but pleasantly so. I was happy too, despite the mysterious voice in the back of my mind that kept insisting that there was something more, some uncharted avenue I still needed to explore. I told myself it was just the seductive whisper of Hollywood and Harlequin romance novels. Why shouldn't I be satisfied by a romantic partnership based on shared interests in music, books, and politics? Soon the niggling voice was drowned out by the details of venues, invitations, dresses, and flowers. We planned to move to Austin a few weeks after the wedding. Between planning the ceremony and the move, I barely had time to ponder whether I was gay or straight. Then the big day arrived, and I was swept along on a stream of rehearsals, receiving lines, first dances, and long-winded toasts.

Throughout it all, Dad was acting strange. He kept sneaking away to find a pay phone. He was wearing an exquisitely tailored double-breasted suit and mirrored sunglasses that he only removed long enough to walk me down the aisle.

"Alex, I can't see your eyes with those glasses on," said my straightforward college roommate, Anne.

"I know!" Dad said proudly, "They're Armani."

On the dance floor after the ceremony, Dad showed off new moves, raising his arms above his head and shaking his fists in a way that I'd never seen him do before. In fact, I'd rarely seen the Chancellor dance at all before.

"What's up with Dad?" I asked my sister when he snuck off to the pay phone yet again. I was still holding my bridal bouquet of sunflowers and roses.

"Um," Kristen hesitated, as if she couldn't quite believe what she was about to say, "I think Dad has a boyfriend."

It had never occurred to me that the resistance I'd felt in D.C. might have been the last gasp of Dad's decades-long struggle to stay in the closet, a specter of his own shame and ambivalence. The irony was a bit rich for a newlywed with the taste of cake still in her mouth. That night, as I removed my wedding jewelry and tucked it into a special keepsake bag, I also tucked away the part of Dad's big news that might have anything to do with me.

Katy steered the truck past a sign proclaiming Lake Jackson, Texas, as "the land of enchantment." The city of Lake Jackson was originally a planned community for white employees of nearby Dow Chemical. Built on the site of an old plantation, the residential streets are named after languid southern flora: Yaupon, Willow, Jasmine, Wisteria. To the east, Dixie Drive forms the boundary with the city of Clute, which is predominantly Mexican American and working-class white. Further south are the chemical plants and the city of Freeport, which is predominantly black. By 1969, when the Koonce family arrived, only a few streets in

Lake Jackson had been integrated. Katy's dad was part of the first class of coaches at Brazoswood High School, a new, integrated 5A school located on the border between Lake Jackson and Clute.

Katy slowed as we turned onto Willow Drive. We passed Persimmon Lane, then Pansy Path. (I shuddered to think of the teasing doled out to little boys with the bad luck to be born on Pansy.) The houses in this neighborhood were 1960s-era development with a choice of three repeated styles: colonial, California contemporary or Tudor revival. We took a left onto Hyacinth Street. Katy pulled into the driveway of a Tudor model with enormous oak trees and long skeins of Spanish moss swaying in the front yard.

Donna came to the door in a sparkly Christmas sweater, knit pants and marabou-trimmed house slippers. Her platinum hair was as perfect as I'd expected, but I was surprised to see the vigor with which her skinny arms embraced her big lug of a daughter. After a long, dancing hug, she turned to me.

"Hi, darling," she said, in a friendly enough tone, but I could feel her eyes pause appraisingly over my close-cropped hair, which was dyed an uneven old-lady lavender. I'd heard stories of previous girlfriends who'd suffered Donna's frank appraisal, which grew more frank throughout the evening as she consumed her customary cocktail—scotch and water in a 24-oz Styrofoam cup.

We stowed our suitcases in Katy's old bedroom and emerged into the dark, smoke-filled living room. The shades were drawn and Donna was resting in her velour recliner, a neatly folded newspaper in her lap. We took our places on the couch, just as in Katy's coming out story. Donna picked up her reading glasses from the side table and lit a Carlton 120.

"Which way did you come?" she asked, scanning the paper absentmindedly.

"I cut over at East Bernard and then took 1875 to 302," Katy said. I had not been able to keep track of all the back roads and short cuts we'd taken and had only a vague idea that we were somewhere near Houston, but I nodded agreeably.

Suddenly, Donna looked right at me. "*Who* is Prufrock's creator?" she asked.

I was taken aback, and it took me several seconds to realize that she was asking for a crossword answer. "Starts with an E," she prompted. My heart was pounding as if I were back in my qualifying exams.

"Eliot!" I cried, stumbling over my own tongue, "It's T. S. Eliot!"

"E-L-I-O-T?" she asked. "That works."

Soon Katy's brother Blaine and his wife Sherry arrived for dinner. Before we sat down to places laid with Koonce family silver, Donna called everyone into the kitchen to join hands. "Lord, thank you for allowing us to be together once more." I bowed my head as she called upon those who were absent, those who had come before, those whose financial foresight to retain their mineral rights had paid for this meal we were about to consume. About two minutes in, I cautiously raised my eyes. Blaine and Katy were watching me with conspiratorial smiles. They knew that the length and superciliousness of the average Donna Koonce prayer could cause innocent bystanders to be seized with fits of giggles. I pressed my lips together and trained my eyes back on the tan kitchen tile.

After dinner, Donna returned to the recliner and we took up our place on the couch. I was feeling pretty good about the visit so far. I had supplied the correct crossword answer and had managed not to laugh inappropriately during grace. I had even managed to strike up a conversation about mystery novels with Katy's dad, who was a man of very few words. Now the starchy Southern food had made me sleepy, and I was just about to doze off for a few seconds when I realized that Katy and her mom were having a fight. It all happened so quickly; one minute they were talking about property taxes and the next minute they were digging into buried reserves of anger and reproach.

"I'd have a lot more money if I hadn't spent so much bailing you out of trouble," Donna said accusingly, taking a pull on her scotch.

"No one forced you to come to my rescue, Mother," Katy said loudly. "If you'd had better boundaries, I probably wouldn't have been so messed up."

At that moment, I wanted nothing more than to melt into the scratchy brown couch. *That's it*, I thought, *the visit's ruined. We'll have to go home.* But while I was mentally packing the suitcases, mother and daughter were already laughing at themselves.

"You sound like a therapist," Donna said wryly.

"I am a therapist," Katy smiled. "Remember, you paid for my education?"

In a matter of seconds, they had moved on to lighter topics and were once again enjoying each other's company. I couldn't believe it. In my own family, open conflict was to be avoided at all costs. Watching Katy and Donna taught me how unrooted I was, how every little storm could make me feel like I'd been felled.

My parents never fought in front of me. Then, shortly after my eleventh birthday, Mom and Dad called a family meeting in the living room. We had moved to Houston a couple of years earlier for Dad's job, and my parents left the last vestiges of their old hippy furniture behind in Indiana. Now my sister and I settled carefully into pristine white couches at the center of a sprawling modern ranch house. After a few awkward pleasantries, my parents dropped a bombshell: they were getting divorced.

They offered the usual platitudes: *we still really love each other, it's not your fault, it's natural to have lots of feelings about what's happening.* Then they informed us that we were going to the symphony that night and we needed to wrap up this little convo in time to get dressed and get ready to leave.

Mom and Dad were not classical music fans. Our family attended the symphony regularly, but I can't remember a time when either of them told me how the music made them feel. Our weekly arts outings were more like an extension of Dad's job, the perfect opportunity for my father to see and be seen by potential donors. On the evening they announced their divorce, I suspect that my parents simply couldn't bear to be alone with our grief. They gambled that a formal occasion would help everyone maintain their composure.

I refused to give them the satisfaction of crying at the allotted moment. I pulled myself up from the couch with all of the pre-teen dignity I could muster and retreated to my bedroom to reorganize. I sorted old toys into a pile for Goodwill with ruthless efficiency, repeating *I will not let them see me cry* over and over in my head.

My sister Kristen, who was only eight, started crying and could not stop, but my parents did not relent. They stuffed her sobbing body into a dress and loaded us all into the car. When we arrived at the theater, she calmed down long enough for us to get to our seats like some semblance of a happy family, but during the symphony—which was long and boring—Kristen started to cry again. The evening's program featured a choral performance, and a hefty blonde soprano with a huge feather in her hair was singing an endless solo in a foreign language. As she sang, she reached her hand toward some unseen object.

"She's singing 'birdseed, birdseed, birdseed,'" my mother whispered into Kristen's ear, trying to cajole the tears away. It wasn't that funny, but my mother kept repeating it, as if any moment, through the tears and the snot, my sister would break into a smile and everything would be okay.

A few weeks later, Mom packed up and moved to Arizona to begin business school. At the end of the summer, she came back with a borrowed pick-up truck and loaded our belongings in the back. We would return to Dad at Christmastime, but just now a hurricane was blowing in from the Gulf. We had to hightail it out of Houston to stay ahead of the storm. I looked back down the driveway to see him looking strangely forlorn without his suit and tie. Big, fat raindrops were beginning to fall, blooming into dark stains across his white t-shirt. In an instant, everything I had known about family life was washed away.

Since my family had moved around a lot, I'd never really had the experience of bringing a lover back to my childhood bedroom. When Katy and I were ensconced in her old double bed, she told me the story of the "Think Pink" baby shower and pointed to where her pink dresser had once stood. It was getting late now, but we could still hear Donna puttering around the kitchen. Katy told me that, when the moon was out, Donna would slide on her house shoes and shuffle out to the moist grass behind the house. There, with a cigarette in one hand, she'd unload her troubles to a personal God—a confection of Father, Son, and pagan moon Goddess. She prayed for all her many grandchildren. She prayed for patience with her husband. She prayed for the social life of her cross-dressing neighbor. For the success of her housekeeper's daughter's quinceañera. Most of all, she prayed for her adult children, that they would find peace and stability before she had to leave them.

Saying your prayers to the moon is pretty risqué stuff in a town where the Baptists still believe that Methodists go to hell. But Donna wasn't shy about it. If the moon was particularly big and beautiful, she'd come inside, pour another drink, and then call friends and family. Katy said it wasn't unusual to hear the phone ring at 11 p.m. "I want you to go outside and look at that moon," she'd evangelize. Then she'd fill your ear with everything she'd been praying about—especially if it had to do with you. Just in case her intercession with the moon didn't work, she was going to take every earthly opportunity to let you know exactly what she thought you should do with your life.

I was uneasy with the prospect of allowing so much directness into my life, but I decided that I could trust the authenticity of Donna's emotions. When she hugged me goodbye at the end of the visit, I could honestly feel the love flowing towards me. She told me how very, very grateful she was that Katy had found me.

"Thank you, darlin'," she whispered in my ear. "Thank you."

CHAPTER 5

———— ⌘ ————

Home

As SOON AS MY year of teaching in frigid Pennsylvania was over, I packed up all my stuff and returned to Austin. Katy and I moved into the top half of the big yellow house and immediately covered the pristine white walls in bright, retro shades of aqua and orange. When the former tenant, the New Age aesthetician, saw our test patches on the walls, she literally cringed. "I can't look," she said, as she pulled the last of her feng shui mirrors from above the back door and hurried away.

Down below, Jim painted his new bachelor pad in self-consciously masculine shades of khaki and tan. He hung his hammock in the backyard and installed his post-divorce hot tub under the stairs that led to our back porch. Sometimes, when we came home from the movies or seeing friends, Jim would be relaxing in the tub, and we'd have a little chat before saying goodnight.

As a therapist, Jim was adept at probing for a person's backstory. As an introvert, I appreciated the way he could cut to the chase without wasting a lot of time on small talk. After a few neighborly dinners together, it was clear we had more in common than I'd initially imagined. We both had high-achieving dads, and we'd both been expected to follow a similar career trajectory. Jim's brothers were doctors and lawyers. In choosing social work school, Jim had sailed off his family's map of career prestige. Later that summer, when I accepted a job as a research associate at the University of Texas, it felt like Jim and I were sailing in the same boat.

On the first day of my new job, I hit the snooze button and stayed in bed, staring at the shadows cast by the morning sun filtering through

Venetian blinds. In my mind, I could hear the lyrics to an old Smiths song: "I was looking for a job and then I found a job, and heaven knows I'm miserable now." I was relieved to have gainful employment, but I dreaded returning to the school where I'd graduated with grand plans only a year before.

I had almost convinced myself to go back to sleep for another 10 minutes when Katy's cell phone rang. She felt around on the nightstand until she found it and flipped it open.

"Hey...Uh-huh. What?" She sat up and threw back the sheets. "I'll call you back."

It was Jim. He was calling to say that an airplane had flown into the World Trade Center. I thought he must be confused or mistaken, but soon Katy and I were glued to the television, feeling helpless and stricken as we watched disaster unfold.

My concerns about my career seemed to belong to another lifetime. A crater had opened between this moment and the past, and it was impossible to know the size of the gap. Like an automaton, I got dressed and went into the office. It was already midday, and I wasn't sure if I was still expected or if the university would even be open for business. I just wanted to get away from the looping footage of planes colliding and bodies falling. I just wanted to do something purposeful, however small.

In the days that followed, my job was like a life raft. I clung to the most perfunctory tasks, grateful for the sense of order and accomplishment. When the workday was done, I headed to the grounds of the Texas capitol to be with other people. At first there were vigils for the dead, but those gatherings soon turned to rallies against the vilification of Muslims and the rush to retaliation.

The knee-jerk patriotism of the days and weeks after 9/11 made my blood boil. When George W. Bush spoke of "the war on terror" and urged Americans to go shopping, I wanted to punch a wall or scream until my voice was hoarse. I was so angry that Katy gently queried whether my political outrage might be a defense against powerlessness.

"Ugh, you therapists!" I cried in frustration. "Why do you always have to personalize everything?"

The next evening, I parked my car in downtown Austin, a few blocks away from the capitol. As I walked toward the capitol gates, the cracked and buckled sidewalk seemed to twist before my eyes, like the ground was literally shifting under my feet. Suddenly, my breath began to come fast and hard, and my eyes welled up. I saw Katy standing at the corner of Congress and 11th, and I ran to her, bursting into tears the second I reached her side.

"I'm just so scared," I sobbed.

"It's okay," she said, wrapping her arms around me. "Sh-sh-sh-sh, it's okay."

I could hear a bullhorn in the background. The rally was starting, and people were moving all around us, but I was loathe to leave our embrace. I knew Katy was every bit as powerless as I was, but I wanted to believe, just for a moment, that her strength would keep me safe.

One afternoon, not long after my outburst on the street, I heard my new co-workers murmuring about a coming storm. My office was nestled in the bunker-like bowels of the undergraduate library. By four o'clock, I could hear the closing of doors and the shuffling of feet all up and down the corridor. The motherly administrative assistant poked her head in the door.

"It's fixin' to rain hard," she said. "You might want to get a head start on the parking garage."

"I'll head out soon," I said. I was combing through the university catalog, methodically tabulating every course that might relate to the new curriculum I was designing. I didn't want to knock off for the day until I was done, but when a clap of thunder shook my basement abode, I knew I had waited too long. By the time I reached my car, my clothes were soaked and the sky was inky black. I pulled cautiously onto Guadalupe Street, but made it only a few blocks south before the traffic lights went out.

Stuck in stop-and-go traffic, unable to see more than a few yards ahead of me through sheets of rain, I turned the radio dial from station to station. All the weather news was about the rural counties surrounding Austin. Meanwhile, downtown, trees were bending in the wind, and I struggled to remember what I'd learned about tornado safety. Should I remain in my car? Or abandon it and try to find shelter in one of the deserted-looking businesses that lined the street? In the wake of 9/11, I couldn't judge whether I was experiencing an ordinary Central Texas storm or being swept along toward some fresh disaster.

After 45 minutes of slow, panicked driving, I finally pulled into the driveway of the big yellow house. Light was shining out of the upstairs kitchen like a beacon in the night. I ran up the slippery outdoor stairs, and Jim met me at the door with a towel. Katy was at the stove, stirring a big, steaming pot of chicken and dumplings. It seemed I'd arrived just in time for dinner. They installed me on the couch in a nest of blankets, and we three ate together in our cozy living room. When the lights went out, somewhere around my second bowl of dumplings, we lit candles and kept on talking.

In the flickering candlelight, Jim relayed what he'd heard from our former real estate agent, who had been in a hotel in lower Manhattan on 9/11 and had walked across the Brooklyn Bridge with throngs of terrified people. We argued about mundane things, like the relative merits of canned peas vs. fresh peas in chicken and dumplings. I recited a rhyme about peas that I'd learned from my grandfather: "I eat my peas with honey, I've done it all my life. It does taste kind of funny, but it keeps them on my knife!"

With the storm howling outside, and war looming in the larger world, home seemed almost unreal, like a stage set of "home." And yet, despite its uncanniness, it was comforting—and Jim was unquestionably part of that comfort. I was glad I'd learned to appreciate him as part of our budding family, especially when the world was shifting too quickly under our feet.

CHAPTER 6

Blood Brothers

IN THE MONTHS THAT followed 9/11, the U.S. invaded Afghanistan, President Bush created the Orwellian-sounding Office of Homeland Security, and a color-coded terrorist risk advisory system cast an orange and red glow of anxiety over everyday life. The President made his notorious "axis of evil" speech. War with Iraq loomed on the horizon.

In short, it seemed like a terrible time to have a baby.

I was reminded of a question that I had always wanted to ask my father. Dad had retired from university leadership and now taught graduate seminars in higher education administration. We spoke on the phone several times a week so that I could give him the blow-by-blow of my job in the provost's office at UT, but today I had something more personal to discuss.

"Dad, when you and Mom decided to have me, did you ever worry that it was a really terrible time to bring a child into the world?" Even on the phone I could visualize the way he closed his eyes and tilted his head forward when I asked him about the past. "I mean, MLK and Bobby Kennedy had been assassinated, there were the Kent State shootings, secret bombings in Cambodia..." I could have gone on, but I hoped he had the general idea.

"Hmm..." Dad paused for a moment. "I don't think so. No."

In the tradition of heterosexuals everywhere, I decided not to think too much about getting pregnant. Straight people had babies because they got carried away in the backseat of a car, or a condom broke, or just because they thought they were supposed to. If Katy thought having a baby was a good idea, then it seemed like a good idea to me too. I was fascinated by her openness to new experiences, and when I was with her, I felt open too. Besides, I was already committed. Before she even came to visit me in Pennsylvania, she'd made it very clear that she wasn't interested in anyone who wasn't interested in having a baby. Now she was nearing 40. She knew that hepatitis C could steal a decade or more from her lifespan. We needed to get busy.

But it wasn't that easy. First we had to figure out *how* we were going to get pregnant. Katy was interested in finding a known donor. "It could be so cool, babe. Our kid will have another adult in their life. Maybe that person could become part of our family, like an uncle or something."

This was precisely why I gravitated toward an anonymous sperm bank. It was more expensive, but simpler—no strings attached. Another adult seemed like an unnecessary entanglement. What if we didn't get along? What if our hypothetical child preferred our hypothetical donor? What if the donor decided to exercise his paternity rights and take our child away someday? I didn't think I could bear it.

I spent hours on sperm bank websites, hoping to find a musically inclined, extroverted donor who would win Katy over to my point of view. I combed the records, searching for Katy's combination of strong jaw, brown hair and green eyes until I started to feel like a Nazi scientist. What was most important to me? SAT scores? Artistic ability? Height? Was I having a baby or building an übermensch? The longer I wrestled with these questions, the more the potential donors began to seem like columns on a spreadsheet instead of real people.

Then Katy brought in the big guns: Friends who had been adopted began to offer their testimonies to me. Some had found their birth parents, some hadn't—but they all spoke of a deep desire to know who they had come from.

"If you're going to go the sperm bank route," one adopted friend said, "at least pick a donor who's open to being contacted. Just in case they have questions. Give the kid some options."

This argument was like kryptonite to my resolve. I had spent hours pondering the circumstances of my birth—and I actually knew my parents. The fact that my parents were divorced, combined with the fact that my dad was gay, made my family of origin like a jigsaw puzzle with a few missing pieces. Why did they get married? What did they see in each other? How was I like them? In what ways was I different? I had a reputation as something of a navel-gazer in my family, and I wondered if any child of mine would have the same inclination. How could I deny him or her the right to ruminate on his or her roots?

Now my instincts swung in the opposite direction. Why not ask one of Katy's brothers to be our donor? Then our kid would be a real Koonce, with access to the fabulous Koonce family mythology. The Koonces were amazing storytellers. The Koonces were musical. The brothers were tall and handsome and had full heads of hair! And, if Donna's decades of smoking and drinking and Katy's years of drug abuse were any indication, it seemed like the Koonces were built from pretty sturdy stock.

As if the whole thing had been my idea from the start, Katy willingly followed my lead, but we immediately faced yet another tricky decision: Should we ask Katy's charismatic brother, Cowboy Blaine, who already had enough kids scattered across East Texas to start his own 4H chapter? Katy's mother needed a spiral notebook just to remember all of their names and birthdays. We would have been assured of Blaine's fertility, but he seemed busy with his own nontraditional family project. Plus, I worried that he was a touch too charismatic. I didn't want to share the parental spotlight. So we asked Katy's more introverted brother, Phil. And he turned us down, in his taciturn way, without any explanation.

Katy was hurt, but perhaps not too surprised. She and Phil were ten years apart, and they'd never been terribly close. Still, it was hard not to read some kind of judgment in his refusal. Did he think there was something wrong in our desire to make a family? Was he concerned that we'd be bad parents and that he'd end up shouldering some unwanted responsibilities? The day after Katy received Phil's politely worded refusal, she plopped down on the living room couch, dialed her best friend Brian in Michigan, and proceeded to pour out the whole unhappy story.

On the other end of the phone line, Brian said, "Well, I won't be too hurt if you don't ask me." Katy brushed off this polite sympathy gesture and went on talking about how disappointed she was to be denied by her own flesh and blood. When it was time to get off the phone, Brian made what was, for an emotionally understated straight guy, a bold plea: "I guess I won't be too sad if you don't pick me."

Unfortunately, that kind of subtlety barely registers on the scale of lesbian processing. They said *bye* and *love you* and hung up the phone. Then Katy sat on the couch for a moment, as if gathering her energies to continue the sperm search. Suddenly her face lit up. "I think Brian actually *wants* to be our donor!"

Katy had always known that she wanted kids, and Brian had always promised that he'd be ready to donate when the time came. But that was back in the eighties, when they lived together in a derelict shack on the swampy Texas coast. Both were recently returned from seeking their fortunes in Hollywood. Brian had travelled west with his hair metal band, Slash Wildly, to make a name in the seedy clubs on the Sunset Strip. Katy had set out for Hollywood to become a movie star—and to come out as a lesbian somewhere far away from small-town Texas. In the end, they'd both wound up hungry, homeless, and addicted to drugs. Each, independently of the other, had finally gotten desperate enough to come back home to mom and dad.

They may have slunk back home with their tails between their legs, but their hair was standing tall. With tight pants, ripped t-shirts, ratted hair, and rows of black plastic bracelets, they didn't look like anyone else in Lake Jackson, Texas. On MTV, bands like Poison, Twisted Sister and Aerosmith were celebrating a new era of American androgyny, but scarves and lace gloves was not a look you saw on straight men (or butch lesbians) in a town where high school football games were the main social event. (In one of my favorite pictures from this era, Brian is wearing a fedora, white lace tights, and a jock strap.) When they first spotted each other from across the bar at a local club, Katy and Brian had the same thought: "Whoa, that dude looks like me."

They became inseparable and lived together through bands, bar fights, break-ups, rock-bottoming, and getting clean. Eventually, in the early nineties, they moved to Austin together. By the time they parted ways as roommates, Katy was starting social work school and Brian was getting married to a Midwestern girl from Michigan. Over the years, they remained close, but neither of them knew whether his promise to help Katy make a family had any meaning in their new worlds.

As it turned out, Brian's willingness to have a cotton swab inserted in his urethra was a solemn testament to the value of his word. We needed our future donor to submit to an extensive array of medical tests, and in spring 2002, Brian left a message on Katy's phone: "Dude, I took a Q-tip for you!"

While we waited for Brian's test results to come back, we planned another wedding. This ceremony would be no more legally binding than the first, but it would involve our friends and family as witnesses to our commitment. Since Brian would be traveling to Austin for the wedding, it would also be our first chance to try to conceive.

CHAPTER 7

❧

Look at That Moon

In 1997, THE GUERRILLA art duo Dyke Action Machine created a poster with an image of two brides surrounded by wedding gifts. "Is it worth being boring for a blender?" the headline queried. At the bottom was the answer: "Gay marriage: You might as well be straight."

In 2002, these words still pretty much summed up our friends' feelings about marriage.

Politically, I was sympathetic to this critique. I'd been reading cultural critics like Lauren Berlant, who argued that a certain version of white, middle class, heterosexual domesticity had become synonymous with citizenship and that our national obsession with family life conveniently redefined inequality as personal pathology rather than social problem.

And yet...Katy had been out for twenty years longer than I had. She lived every day on the front lines of gender indeterminacy, had to deal with all manner of shit from people who didn't know what she was or how to treat her, and she hungered for this particular form of recognition. It seemed cruel to deny her, especially after I found the perfect dress at Goodwill for $5.99—a sparkly white polyester minidress that was right out of Priscilla Presley's closet.

As a compromise, we decided to create a ceremony that would celebrate friends and community. Rather than having bridesmaids and groomsmen, we would include all of the people who had been our social support networks over the years. We planned to recognize each one with a few words about what they meant to us. For me that meant publicly acknowledging my sister, plus a few close friends from high school, college and graduate school. For Katy that meant honoring her brothers and a large crew of best friends and ex-girlfriends.

Katy's enthusiasm was infectious and overwhelming at the same time. We set the date for her fortieth birthday, and she got right down to inviting everyone she'd ever known—from the folks in our old therapy group (definitely against the rules) to the supermarket cashier whom she remembered from back in the day at the gay bars. I trembled to think how we would seat and feed them all, but, in addition to wedding guests, Katy also had a seemingly endless supply of old buddies with small businesses or special talents—everything from catering to graphic design to party rentals—and she wasn't the least bit shy about asking for help. Her fearlessness in this regard was a revelation to me. I had always thought of friendship as a delicately balanced give-and-take, and I was careful never to ask too much. Katy's theory was that people could always say no, but they might actually enjoy helping and being part of our big queer celebration.

In the end, it was the communal aspect of the wedding preparations that won me over. I was afraid of sliding into a private realm of bridal registries and blenders that was virtually indistinguishable from heterosexual life. And the wedding did seem to require innumerable trips to Home Depot and Party Pig and other stores that made me feel like I was a sheep blandly following George Bush's exhortation to shop, shop, shop my cares away. But, on the flip side, the wedding afforded the chance to work side by side with a bunch of amazing queer artists and artisans who were really excited to help make it happen.

When it came time to make the wedding invitations, I knew exactly who I wanted to design them, but I hardly dared to dream that she would say yes. Terri Lord was the drummer for a bunch of beloved local bands. She was also a talented visual artist, and her campy collages could be seen on posters for all kinds of queer and feminist events around Austin. Katy already knew Terri (of course) and happily invited her over for a design consultation. I was surprised that this super-cool artist listened intently to the hokey story of our romance and eagerly contributed ideas for an eerie piece of mail art that would honor our first ceremony in Lily Dale. At the end of our meeting, I broached the question of cost.

"What's your usual rate for design?"

Terri had long blonde hair that often fell across her face. "Don't worry about it," she said, smiling with embarrassment as she tucked a strand behind her ear.

"No, seriously. We have to pay you. This could be a lot of work."

"I'm just honored to be a part of it," she said, flashing a sweet smile and glancing back and forth between Katy and me.

After that initial meeting, Terri and I talked on the phone. In between conversations about color saturation and printer's bids, she told me snippets of stories about crazy nights with famous musicians and legendary shows at The Electric Lounge and Liberty Lunch. I'd been in the audience for some of those shows! I wanted to pinch myself, but I also felt scared that she would realize that I wasn't really all that cool.

I was still struggling to fit in with Katy's queer community of musicians and artists. Without a professor job, I didn't feel like I had an identity or creative outlet, so I started making a 'zine called *Domestic Queer*, which featured vintage clip art, ironic housekeeping tips, and interviews about nontraditional living arrangements. With my reporter's notebook in hand, I felt less shy, and the interview format provided a reassuring protocol for interactions.

One of the first people I interviewed for *Domestic Queer* was Gretchen Phillips. In the queer music world, Gretchen was a living legend. She'd been a founding member of Two Nice Girls—the first avowedly lesbian band I'd ever heard on the radio. In grad school, I'd gone to see her perform and had come to treasure one of her solo albums. Gretchen's long-time girlfriend was my former dissertation director, Dr. Ann Cvetkovich—a formidable presence in the field of feminist studies. I'd visited their house many times, but I'd always been slightly intimidated. Gretchen had a way of talking that made everything sound incredibly ironic, and she had no tolerance for small talk. If I said something innocuous like, "Have a good time," she'd answer, "Well, I certainly intend to try. I rarely set out to have a bad time," which made me feel presumptuous for trying to tell her what kind of time to have.

When it came time for our interview, I arrived at Gretchen's backyard studio with a list of what I hoped were substantive and interesting questions. For starters, I wanted to ask about her backyard art studio, which was known as the "pod." I was intrigued that Ann and Gretchen's domestic life revolved around separate work spaces.

I also wanted to learn more about a new batch of cover songs that Gretchen had recorded with her friend Dave Driver.

"These songs—I feel like, if anyone else had covered them, they would be campy. But I get the feeling that your versions are really sincere."

"Yeah, I don't really do insincerity," she answered, looking straight at me with clear, piercing eyes. I was glad to be able to hide behind the video camera I used to record my interviews. I fumbled with the lens, trying to bring Gretchen's face into clearer focus. I was blushing madly because I realized that I'd pegged her all wrong.

Of all of our friends, Gretchen was perhaps the most vocal critic of gay marriage. Her band Girls in the Nose actually recorded a song called "Weddings Are Icky." She'd also made it clear that she wasn't happy about the idea that Katy and I might have a baby.

"I know exactly what's going to happen," she told us gloomily. We were on our way to a concert, and Gretchen was riding in the backseat. She rested her forehead poutily against the back of the driver's seat. "I'll never see you guys anymore." It was hard not to be touched by her disappointment.

Despite her skepticism about marriage, Gretchen was incurably romantic. I loved her songs and stories about the way she'd wooed "the Lady C," as she sometimes called Dr. Cvetkovich. She was a fervent believer in love and forgiveness and compassion, and when she got going, she could really preach. One night we were hanging out with Gretchen and the Lady C at the Star Seeds diner. Gretchen was riffing on one of her favorite themes, the healing power of togetherness, and I had a sudden inspiration.

"Katy," I leaned across the torn leather banquette. "Maybe we should ask Gretchen to perform our ceremony!" It was an audacious, out-of-left-field idea. I figured we'd discuss it in private. But a few minutes later, as we were saying goodbyes in the parking lot, Katy blurted out "Gretchen, we think you should officiate at our wedding."

Gretchen hesitated. I could tell she was torn between her aversion to same-sex marriage and her pleasure at being asked. "Well," she said, smiling and twisting her crazy mop of silver-gray hair, "I have always wanted to start my own church."

From that point forward, Gretchen took her role as officiant very seriously. We met several times for dinner and pre-marital counseling, and she asked hard questions.

"Do you really believe in the whole 'til death do us part thing?" she asked one night over veggie burgers at our kitchen table.

"Well..." I didn't want to hurt Katy's feelings, but my own mother had been married three times, and I was already divorced once myself. There was no way for me to talk about eternity without feeling like a hypocrite. "Let's focus on the present," I said diplomatically.

"I just want to get up in front of all those people and say 'I'll never fuckin' leave you and I'll love you 'til the day I die," Katy said, slapping the table for emphasis. A warm glow spread from my heart to my head to my cheeks. Sometimes it was hard to believe that such a straightforward person could love a skeptical curmudgeon like myself.

"Why don't you just leave that part up to us?" I asked Gretchen. "You don't have to say anything about death or eternity—we'll cover it in our own ways in our vows."

Gretchen was also concerned that we'd chosen "The Origin of Love" from *Hedwig and the Angry Inch* as our procession song. Based on a tale from Plato's *Symposium*, the song posits that there were once three sexes, and each sex had a distinctly dual nature. The "children of the sun" had two male halves, the "children of the earth" had two female halves:

And the children of the moon
Were like a fork shoved on a spoon.
They were part sun, part earth
Part daughter, part son.

According to the story, these dyadic humans were very powerful and threatening to the Gods. In order to put them in their proper place, Zeus split each human whole in half with a lightening bolt. From that point forward, human beings were destined to spend their lives searching for their missing halves and trying—in vain, perhaps—to regain their original feeling of wholeness.

"Do you really feel like you have some kind of primal lack? Do you feel like you need to get married to become whole?" Gretchen's obvious bewilderment and disapproval was making me lose my appetite.

"No," I said, setting down my veggie burger. "It's not that. It's just…" I felt exposed under Gretchen's direct gaze. I knew my fake smile would never fly with her, but I was scared to put words to my deepest feelings and beliefs. Was it fetishizing to admit that Katy's masculinity with a twist—like a fork shoved on a spoon—was more compelling to me than any homogenous gender with a matching inside and outside? Was it reductive to believe that our queer genders might complement each other? When we made love, I had the thrilling feeling that we were making our own world. Maybe it wasn't destiny with a capital D, but it felt wildly creative, exquisitely attuned, and uniquely *us*.

"It's just that…I feel like we were meant to be together, like we just fit." I took a bite of veggie burger and forced it down over the lump in my throat. The whole thing sounded so mushy and mystical when I was forced to say it out loud.

In the months after 9/11, everyone was kind of hunkered down, but our housemate Jim had gone further down in the hole than most. He had broken up with his girlfriend, his private practice had dwindled, and he spent most of his time alone in his room. When he emerged, he looked pale, skinny, scruffy, and sad.

The wedding was to take place in our shared backyard, and the requisite preparations seemed to bring Jim back to the land of the living. He bought a bunch of flagstones and started extending the back patio, digging into the hard caliche dirt and placing rocks in an intricate spiral pattern. One night, as we were wrapping up our yard chores for the evening, Jim asked about the dress code for the wedding. "Dress code?" Katy asked. "There's no dress code. Hell, half the people will probably be in drag." She was exaggerating, but Jim took this comment to heart. From that moment forward, he acted as though he had a personal responsibility to appear in high drag at our wedding.

In the meantime, Brian had passed the STD test, and we were moving closer to insemination. Since Brian wasn't a big fan of air travel, we decided that he would come to Austin for the wedding and leave a "deposit" at the local sperm bank during the same trip. If the timing was right, we would also do a home insemination with fresh sperm while he was in town.

So many friends pitched in for the wedding. Stife chose the flowers, John wrapped our trees in hundreds of sparkly white lights, and Mark edited a video for the multimedia portion of the celebration. Amidst all this frenetic activity, Jim rented a Harley. Then he called the restaurant where we were hosting our rehearsal dinner and asked whether he could ride the Harley into the lobby of the restaurant to make his entrance.

Admittedly, this seemed a little odd. My friends from high school and college were coming to town. Katy was juggling her three best friends from junior high, plus her aging parents who weren't accustomed to traveling. Most of these people had never met Jim, so his grand entrance wouldn't really make a splash. However, we were so busy getting everyone settled, we hardly had time to think about what was going on in Jim's mind.

Plus, as guests arrived from near and far, something big was happening behind the scenes. Every morning, I logged my temperature in a little notebook by the bed. On the morning of the wedding, my temperature spiked a few tenths of a degree. Katy called Brian at the Holiday Inn where he and his wife were staying. "Dude," she said. "It's time."

A few minutes later, Brian called back. "Do you have any, uh, reading materials?"

"Babe," Katy called into the kitchen, "Do we have any porn?"

"Um, I think we might have a tape called *Dicks Ahoy*."

"We only have gay sailor porn," she reported. "You might want to pick something up on the way."

An hour later, Brian was walking down the driveway, smoking a cigarette and sheepishly clutching a brown paper bag. We welcomed him, and then stayed downstairs chatting with Jim so that Brian could have the upper apartment to himself for a while.

Before long, our sperm donor said an embarrassed round of goodbyes, and Katy was standing in our bedroom with a small jar of fresh semen. "It doesn't look anything like *Something About Mary*," she said, indignantly. "It's way more watery than I thought." She did a little jig with the jar. "Leettle swimmers, leettle, leettle swimmers!"

"Hurry up," I said. "I don't want the little swimmers to die out here in the open air." Katy sucked the liquid into a plastic syringe. I pulled back the sheet and spread my legs. It wasn't clinical, but it wasn't exactly sexy to be naked with my wife and her best friend's sperm. I let Katy do the honors, and she shot Brian's wad toward my cervix. I laid in the bed for a good long while, hoping to give some lucky sperm a chance to find an egg. After a while I had to get up. It was time to get hitched.

Outside, our backyard was already a hive of activity. In one corner, a group of dykes were raising the stage where the bands would play. In the garage, our friend Rachael rustled around until she found an old sheet and a couple of bamboo poles, which she sewed together into a giant screen for our video projections. Pretty soon, Brian returned with his guitar, and he and Blaine started practicing the blues numbers that they planned to play after the first band—a super group that included many of Katy's former band mates—finished their set.

My mom was there too, making last-minute runs for cocktail napkins and extra cups. When it was time for me to get dressed, she came upstairs to help. I slipped on the dress, white fishnets, white vinyl go-go boots and a pair of mod teardrop earrings that I had stolen from Mom's jewelry box as a teenager. The whole ensemble was like the drag queen version of her 1967 wedding outfit. I hoped she could sense the homage, because I was far too nervous to put it in words. I started to put my makeup on, but my hands were shaking. "Mom," I said plaintively, "can you do this?" In my teen years, she had waged a one-woman crusade against my beloved black eyeliner, but now she patiently applied layer after layer. I was grateful for her steady hands and unflagging support. You'd never guess that there was anything unusual about a lesbian wedding—or that this was the second wedding I'd put my family through in less than a decade.

None of us had ever been part of a wedding like this before, though. When Katy and I walked out the door in our wedding clothes, the backyard was twinkling with tiny white lights. More than 150 people were milling around on a hot July night, and they all turned to look at us. In between the camera flashes, I saw the faces of all the people who had helped make the celebration possible. *How am I ever going to repay them?* I wondered as we circulated through the crowd. Then the band started playing "The Origin of Love," and Gretchen's haunting, vulnerable voice filled the air. Katy and I made our way through the crowd to the patio. Twenty of our most special people were already seated behind us, including my mom in white voile and Donna Koonce in a stunning black sequined number. Jim was a few seats away in a blonde wig, fringed biker-chick t-shirt and denim mini skirt.

As the band finished playing, Gretchen took her place between us and welcomed the guests. "This is a very brave thing that Katy and Paige are doing here today. They're being really public about their mushy feelings. It's a celebration of tears." I looked at Katy, so handsome in her rock-n-roll frock coat. Tears were already welling in her eyes, which looked at me with so much love and joy and gratitude that tears began to slide down my own cheek.

Like a preacher with a piece of scripture, Gretchen directed the congregation's attention to the lyrics of "The Origin of Love."

"I sat down with Katy and Paige and this was my impression of the song's meaning for them: they believe that spirit resides in the relationships of things, inside the act of actually relating. When we know that that is what we're doing, we are responding to and affecting other beings by our presence in the world, we can realize the realm of the spiritual." Gretchen was on a roll, and she took a deep breath before delving deeper into her theme.

Suddenly, there was a stirring in the front row. Donna Koonce stood up and reached for the microphone. The audience gasped. It was like the "speak now or forever hold your peace" moment in a soap opera, when someone stands up to say why the happy couple should not be joined in holy matrimony. "Your turn is coming," Gretchen scolded. Donna, undeterred, grabbed the mic and pointed to the sky. Then she spoke, slowly and Southernly, to the crowd. "I. Want. You...to *look* at that *moon!*" Thus instructed, the entire audience gazed skyward and gasped again. A giant silver orb, a spectacular full moon, was shining its blessing on our nuptials.

When it was my turn to speak, it felt like a recurring dream I had, the one where I was naked in front of a class of expectant students. I was about to verbalize my feelings for each of my closest friends, and I was terrified that my words would be too much—too intimate, too real. But there was no turning back now. I hadn't prepared a plan B. In a shaky, sob-constricted voice, I told my sister that her companionship had kept me sane through the rough patches of childhood. The mic was hot and it kept feeding back, but I plowed ahead, embracing the shrieks and pops as part and parcel of the rawness. With streaming eyes and a level gaze, I reminded my best friend from high school how our shared fantasies of running away to New York had helped me survive the teenage wasteland of the suburbs. I told my friends from college and grad school how much they taught me about work and play. When it was time to acknowledge Katy, I told her that loving her, loving all of her—even the parts that caused her grief and shame—had helped me learn to love the unloved parts of myself. I was weeping now. Mascara and false eyelashes be damned, I didn't care.

When it was Katy's turn, my tears continued to flow. In typical Katy fashion, she'd brought together friends from all walks of life—from white, urban art nerds to devout South Texas Mexican Catholics. She thanked her brothers for teaching her how to be a man, and she thanked her old softball buddies for sticking by her through thirty years of friendship. From her hometown of Lake Jackson, she recognized three generations of homegrown butches who had nurtured one another across the years.

When she came to me, Katy's eyes were glistening with tears. I don't remember her exact words, but I know I felt more seen, more known and acknowledged, than I had ever been before in my life. She spoke in tearful, husky tones, gently coaxing the microphone to behave. At the end, she covered the mic and shouted for all to hear, "And I'll never fucking leave you, and I'll love you 'til the day I die!"

After the cheers from the crowd died down, Gretchen pronounced us wife and wife and invited us to "kiss the bride." When I looked up from our long and passionate kiss, I noticed that several other folks in the wedding party had taken advantage of the opportunity to make out with their dates too.

"Now there's time," Gretchen said, shaking off the steamy embrace of the Lady C, "for people in the audience to say a few words to Katy and Paige."

In order to avoid awkward pauses, we had asked a few friends to come prepared with words. Before any of our peers could unfurl crumpled notes or well-worn Neruda poems from their pockets, my dad stood up. At sixty-one, he was still tall and lithe in his designer jeans and silver V-neck summer sweater. I held my breath for a moment, because I knew he'd sipped a few flutes of champagne before the ceremony, but he stepped gracefully across the patio, took the mic from Gretchen, and straightened the cord with a little flick of his arm. Next he turned away from the PA, which effectively silenced the feedback but also meant that he was facing away from me and Katy and most of the audience. Addressing himself to the special guests on the patio, he spoke in the casual tones of a practiced public speaker.

"You know, tonight is really about..."

Oh my God, what was he going to say? Was tonight about love? Friendship? Community? Was he about to wax nostalgic on his little girl growing up? Or was he going to point out—facetiously, but with a bit of an edge—that we had excluded our parents from the ceremony? I felt a twinge of guilt. So many queer people would give the world for their parents' support, and yet here we were, putting chosen family in the spotlight and relegating our parents to the edge of the stage.

"Tonight is really about *mentoring*."

Ah yes, mentoring—that classic theme of wedding toasts since time immemorial. I had to hand it to the Chancellor for discerning that our ceremony was about more than romantic love. However, I happened to know that he had recently given a speech on mentoring at a South Texas community college, and now he treated the assembled guests to polished chestnuts from his long career in higher education. In an instant, I remembered one of the reasons why I needed to put my friends front and center: raw and honest emotional communication was not exactly my family's strong suit.

When Dad was finished, my friend Sandy took the mic. Sandy had been my confidante when I first met Katy, and now she regaled the audience with details of my profound and discombobulating crush. She handed the mic to Dianne, Katy's best friend since eighth grade, who told the wedding guests how she loved to call Katy early in the morning and serenade her with a cheerful rendition of "Good Morning to You."

"Now I have two friends to sing for," she concluded, wiping tears from her eyes. Finally, Jim stood up in his short, short denim skirt and read a heartfelt poem.

My friends' witness marked a transition in my life. Not the traditional transition that a woman makes from her father's family to her husband's family—but a transition from an old way of living to a new community. Tonight, I had revealed so much of myself in word and song and in the requests I'd made to friends and family. Asking for so much had made me feel vulnerable and scared, like jumping blind from a very tall height. I'd been afraid of falling on my face, but instead I'd landed in a safety net of outstretched arms.

CHAPTER 8

Mandala

AFTER THE WEDDING, KATY and I left for a honeymoon trip to Greece. On the shores of Santorini, we filled a toy boat with offerings candy, cigars, a candle, and a tiny plastic baby doll. A friend had instructed us to perform a Santeria fertility ritual, so we lit the candle and asked Yemayá to send us a baby. I was a bit dubious about this blatant act of cultural appropriation, but when the tiny boat travelled far out to sea, we could see the flickering candlelight rising and falling on the waves all the way to the horizon. It seemed like a good sign.

We returned to Texas full of hope. When my period started a few days later, I felt worse for having been so unguarded. Katy had probably told twenty or thirty of her closest friends that we'd done the insemination on our wedding day, and now everyone would know that it didn't work. *Will they think something is wrong with me? Is there something wrong with me?* Despite my best feminist critique, some small part of my brain wondered whether a lack of fertility was a reflection on my ability to love and be loved. On this new frontier of family making, it was sobering to come face to face with old-fashioned shame.

We decided to try again immediately with the frozen sperm that Brian had deposited when he came to town for the wedding. The folks at the sperm bank had cautioned that Brian's motility was low, so Katy and I decided to use all eleven of our vials at once. They arrived at our house in a steel cylinder packed with dry ice. When the thermometer told us the time was nigh, we unpacked the steaming container. The instructions directed us to warm the vials with body heat, so I tucked seven tiny containers in my bra, and Katy packed two in each armpit.

This time around, we were determined to have a more ceremonial aspect to our insemination. I put on The Talking Heads' album *Little Creatures* as our baby-making music and Katy carefully poured all eleven vials into a mason jar. Next, she sucked them up into the syringe, but this time we paused to kiss before she pushed the plunger down. When she was done with sperm delivery, she made sure I had an orgasm. We'd read that the contractions caused the cervix to slurp up more sperm.

Several days later, I turned off the alarm clock and rolled out of bed. On the way to the kitchen for a cup of coffee, something caught my eye. I stepped to the window to check it out. Jim was in the front yard, playing Frisbee with his dog. It was 6 a.m., which seemed a bit odd, but I continued with my morning routine, took a shower, got dressed, packed my satchel and headed downstairs. Jim's car was blocking the driveway, and I walked to the front to ask him to move.

"Paige, Paige!" he said, wiping sweat from his brow. "I'm so glad you're here! You are absolutely the perfect person to be right here at this moment. I've gotta show you the mandala." He gestured in the direction of his white Toyota Tercel.

"Jim, I have to get to work. Can you show me later?"

"It will only take a minute. You've gotta see it. I made a ritual. On a mountain. And then the cops came and they talked to me but they didn't bust me. I had a joint lying in the ashtray but they didn't bust me."

Jim ushered me toward the back of his car. It looked like a child had finger-painted a big circle of mud on the trunk and outlined it with sand and pebbles. "They didn't bust me because I'm the son of God, that's me..." he veered off into a muttered conversation with himself.

Wow, I thought, with a kind of ingrained literary critical detachment. *I can't believe insanity is so cliché.*

"That's a...nice...mandala," I said carefully. "I need to go now." I started to slowly back away. My heart was beating out of my chest, and I wanted to call for help, but I was afraid of setting him off.

"No, no!" he said, "Don't go! I have to show you the card that the cops gave me." He grabbed my wrist and pulled me toward the passenger door.

His touch transmitted a surge of electricity that traveled up my arm and into my chest. I could actually feel adrenaline pumping through my veins. I thought, *this can't be good for the baby.*

At that moment, and in the mania that ensued, Jim knew many things. He knew how to send psychic messages and how to make his dog fly and how to decode the secret signs in the angles of telephone poles.

At that moment, when the madman touched me, I knew one thing. I was pregnant.

In the weeks that followed, Katy and I tried to help Jim in every way we knew how. Katy called their mutual mentor and staged an intervention. When that failed, we called the police psychiatric services. They assumed that Jim was on massive drugs.

"We can't take him unless he's a danger to himself or others," they said, chuckling at his zany antics. They didn't know that Jim had taken to walking into our neighbors' houses—whether or not they were home—and helping himself to "gifts from the universe." One neighbor came home to find Jim's wallet in her laundry room. Another came over to complain because Jim had barged into his living room while he was watching TV. We were more than a little afraid that Jim would get shot by some gun-toting Texas homeowner, and it was a relief when Jim was finally arrested and admitted to the state hospital.

Unfortunately, Jim's health insurance didn't cover mental health care. The doctors at the state hospital medicated him, but they only kept him for five days, which was barely enough time for the meds to begin working. To make matters worse, Jim's family was anxious to push the whole thing under the rug. His dad and brother had flown to Austin while he was in the hospital, but they left a few days later with assurances that Jim would pull it together and get back to work.

By now, a pregnancy test had confirmed that I was, indeed, pregnant. I wanted nothing more than to rest and nest, but our house was literally a mad house. Jim couldn't stop feng-shui-ing everything, and he set up little altars all over the backyard. He was obsessed with flowing water, and he spent hours in the hot tub, despite the late-September heat, getting out only to pour bottles of water over his many makeshift shrines. Despite repeated phone calls from Katy, Jim's family continued to insist that he was on the mend, and Jim became more suspicious every time she tried to intervene.

Eventually he met some high rollers at a strip club and took off with them on a Central American vacation. It was there, in a country with state-funded health care, that he was hospitalized for long enough to begin to come back to reality. When he returned to the United States five weeks later, his family finally accepted that he couldn't go back to work. They made plans for him to move home to the Midwest, and we scrambled to borrow money to buy his half of the house. Jim accepted our modest offer with great reluctance, and the rift that had begun when he was psychotic quickly turned into a permanent break. It was sad and disorienting to lose our friend and housemate in a matter of months, but we barely had time to grieve. The first part of my pregnancy was almost over, and we threw ourselves into preparing for a new member of the family.

CHAPTER 9

Should Waylon Have
Two Mommies?

PREGNANCY MADE ME FEEL really frugal. Maybe it was because we'd unexpectedly acquired Jim's half of the house, or maybe it was some kind of nesting instinct, but I vowed to wear only second-hand maternity clothes, I hoarded hand-me-down onesies, and I opted for the cheapest birthing class I could find.

On the evening of the first meeting, Katy and I parked in one of the hospital surface lots and wandered around until we found the education annex. I was beginning to move like a pregnant woman, and Katy held my arm protectively as we walked down the stairs to a vinyl-tiled basement corridor. In the doorway to the training room, a pasty social worker named Pat was checking off names on a clipboard.

"I'm Paige Schilt," I said. "And this is my wife, Katy."

Pat's eyes traveled from me to Katy and back again.

"Oh, uh-hum, okay." She laughed a nervous, high-pitched laugh. I had the feeling that we'd overloaded her circuits, and I felt annoyed that her social work training hadn't prepared her to make same-sex couples feel more welcome. At the same time, I was aware that we weren't exactly a typical lesbian couple. If she had been reading Katy as a man, I might have startled her when I used the word "wife."

These kinds of interactions happened all the time. Heck, I hadn't been able to decipher the complex puzzle of Katy's gender when I first saw her in Raunchy Reckless and the Amazons. Now that we were

59

together, I could never predict when a stranger would read her as male and when they would read her as female. Katy was usually content to play along with whatever pronouns people assigned her. The one thing she didn't like was when people changed their appraisal in the middle of an interaction. She wanted to protect them from embarrassment, and she also wanted to avoid the anger that sometimes came with it.

Inside the classroom, we found two seats in the circle. On our right were two Latinas—a twenty-something pregnant woman and an older companion. I hoped that they would turn out to be dykes, but they didn't give us the knowing lesbian look. To our left was a young middle-class straight couple of a sort you see around Austin quite a bit. The woman was wearing hand-beaded earrings, and the man looked like maybe he'd been in a band in college before he became an accountant. He gave Katy a curt, dudely nod. *This ought to be interesting*, I thought.

"Welcome Moms and Dads!" Pat had taken her place near the white board at the front of the room. She looked at us and the two women to our right. "...And, uh, partners." Geez, I thought, I know they might not get a lot of queers, but surely they see a lot of pregnant women without a dad in the picture. I sized up the rest of the room to see if anyone else was rolling their eyes. Near the door was a white woman in expensive-looking running tights and running shoes. She looked like the kind of person who would start doing sit-ups in the delivery room, and her husband's hair was coiffed like Texas governor Rick Perry. Definitely Republicans.

At the other side of the circle were two young white couples who seemed to know each other. Something about their behavior—men slouched low in their seats, women giggling over Pat's introduction—made me think that they were attending the class under duress. The women were drinking Sprites and sharing a bag of Funyuns from the vending machine in the hallway. Mrs. Running Tights looked like she was going to spontaneously combust from all the self-righteous energy that she was directing their way.

Pat asked everyone to introduce themselves and explain what they hoped to get out of the class. The women mostly talked about how many months along they were, how they'd been feeling, and whether they were having a boy or a girl. The men said reluctant things like "I'm just here to support her." Most of them looked embarrassed already, and we hadn't even begun to talk about vaginal canals.

When it was my turn, I told the group my name and then proceeded to speak in the first person plural.

"We just found out that we're having a boy. Our due date is May 12," I said, gesturing to include Katy. "It feels really soon, and I'm just hoping to learn more about what to expect in the delivery process." Then, to take some of the pressure off Katy, I decided to introduce her too.

"This is my wife, Katy," I said quickly, smiling and scanning the class.

I couldn't tell how our classmates received this piece of information, but Katy handled the occasion like a pro.

"I'm really looking forward to this class," she said. "Because it's hard, you know, not being the one who's carrying the baby. I want to be as involved as I can, and sometimes it's scary, thinking that she'll be in pain and I won't know how to help." Compared to the other partners, Katy was positively verbose, and I had to smile, because I knew that the therapist part of her just couldn't resist this opportunity for a little psycho-education. She was trying to model to the other dudes how to express feelings and still be manly.

On the second week of birthing class, Pat dutifully broached the topic of circumcision. She gingerly laid out some of the arguments for and against the removal of the foreskin, all the while looking absolutely terrified that someone might express an actual opinion. In the end, she advised us to speak with our OB-GYN about any concerns.

When Katy and I got in the car after class, I was fairly confident that we'd be on the same page, but I wanted to test the waters.

"I can't believe that anyone would cut a newborn baby!"

"Well," Katy said, keeping her eyes on the road, "I can see why some people might do it, you know, just so their kid won't get teased in gym class."

"Times are changing," I said. "More and more parents are deciding not to circumcise. It won't even be a big deal anymore." My sister had dated an anti-circumcision activist in college, and I was basing my argument on a sample of one straight guy, but I hoped I was right.

"Yeah, maybe," Katy replied. I could tell she wasn't quite ready to grant my point. "It's just that I want my son to look like..." she trailed off.

"You want your son's penis to look like your imagined penis?"

"Yeah, kinda," she said sheepishly.

I could tell we were at an impasse, but I wasn't ready to give up. For New Year's, we went to visit our gayest friends, Martin and Richard, in San Francisco. We were hanging out in their baroquely appointed living room when I happened to let slip that we hadn't yet agreed about circumcision.

"Oh my God, *no!*" said Richard.

Both friends were adamant that no gay man in his right mind would want to lose the pleasure potential of his foreskin, a.k.a. nature's masturbation sleeve.

"But," Katy objected, "don't uncircumcised penises look funny, like shriveled carrots?"

I had to shake my head. As a trans-masculine person, Katy was generally much more of a connoisseur of the male physique than I was. But, as a gold star lesbian, her actual experience with unclothed penises was rather limited.

"Honey, it doesn't look any different when it's hard," Martin said.

"It doesn't?" she marveled. I could tell she was starting to come around.

"And if he feels strongly about it, he can always get circumcised later. But he can't get that shit back if you cut it off."

"Let him make the choice," Richard concluded. "He'll thank you for it later."

Katy was nodding her head, and I could tell I'd won the battle. I breathed a big sigh of relief.

After New Year's, we returned to Austin and the start of the 2003 state legislative session. It was shaping up to be a fertile year for anti-gay bills in the Texas legislature. An up-and-coming homophobe named Robert Talton introduced a bill that would ban homosexuals and bisexuals from being foster parents. In his testimony before the State Affairs committee, Talton compared gay parents to pedophiles and suggested that foster children would be better off in orphanages than in "bisexual or homosexual households because that's a learned behavior." Fortunately, in a state with a strong libertarian strain, Talton's bill presented a practical problem: how to determine which of the state's thousands of foster parents might be gay or bisexual. Another bill, Rep. Warren Chisum's The Defense of Marriage Act (DOMA for short), faced no such road bumps. In response to recent developments in California and Vermont, Texas's DOMA enshrined the lone star state's refusal to recognize the legal status of same-sex domestic partnerships or civil unions from other states. Given that President Clinton had signed the federal version of DOMA into law back in 1996, the passage of the Texas state version seemed like a sure thing.

While both of these bills were worrisome, and both contributed to a general feeling of legislative hostility toward our emerging family, it was a lesser-known bill—HB 916—that caused Katy and I to lose the most sleep. Introduced by Rep. Sid Miller from Stephenville, Texas, HB 916 proposed that "a petition for the adoption of a child by more than one person may only be filed by one man and one woman." The bill was aimed at second-parent adoption, which was precisely the legal procedure we hoped to use to secure Katy's legal status as our baby's parent. If it passed in the legislature in the spring, it would become law on September 1, 2003. Due to a six-month waiting period on second-parent adoptions, Katy would miss the opportunity to adopt our child by a narrow two-month window.

"I already love him so much," Katy said, tears welling in her eyes. "I just want to be able to protect him and take care of him—especially if, God forbid, anything ever happened to Paige."

We were sitting in the familiar circle of birthing class, and Katy was continuing her psychoeducational program of displaying masculine-spectrum emotion, but this time with a twist. With the introduction of HB 916 into the sharing circle, Katy was making the political explicitly personal. Her tears were a plea to our fellow prospective parents: feel my pain, identify with my fears, and become an ally. Take a stand against these hateful bills.

Katy was the perfect person to make these kinds of appeals. In spite of her potentially alarming gender ambiguity, Katy's country accent and folksy ways tended to put people at ease. When we went to visit her parents in Lake Jackson, everyone from burly chemical plant workers to purse-lipped church ladies came out to hug her and reminisce about fun times they'd had. Katy could talk about everything from rodeo to the latest reality TV stars, and her self-effacing humor and easy laugh were usually infectious.

But here in the hospital basement, no one reached out to hug her or even met her eyes. At the break, no brave souls came up to tell us that they, too, were outraged by legislative queer bashing. Perhaps people just didn't know what to say. But it felt as if Katy had violated a serious taboo by making politics explicit in birthing class. When the class resumed after break, there were empty seats on either side of us.

On April 6, 2003, Katy's hometown newspaper, *The Brazosport Facts*, ran a front-page story about our family:

It's every mother's nightmare, and one former Lake Jackson resident fears a proposed state law will make it worse for her than for most mothers.

The nightmare starts out the same for Katy Koonce, with a cryptic late night phone call saying her son was in an accident. There is a frantic drive to the hospital, wondering how he is. Then, the twist. A nurse tells Koonce that only family members can visit, so she cannot see her son.

"It really scares me," said Koonce, now an Austin resident. "In a situation like that, the last thing you want to do is be fighting with the people at the hospital."

Should Waylon have two mommies?

Koonce, 40, is not yet a mother, but she will be soon. Her partner, Paige Schilt, is expecting a son, Waylon, at the beginning of May. But Koonce worries that if a proposed bill in the state's House of Representatives passes, she will never be able to legally adopt the boy she considers her son.

A few weeks earlier, Katy and I participated in an LGBT lobby day at the Texas state capitol. I was wearing my one fancy maternity outfit—a black wrap dress that I'd inherited from a friend—and I was determined to work my pregnant girth for all it was worth. When we checked in at the volunteer table, the organizers were excited to learn that Katy had roots in east and southeast Texas. They assigned us to a small group that would visit representatives from Panola and Brazoria counties. To get warmed up, our group decided to hit the Democrats first, and we spoke to a friendly rep from Katy's grandparents' district. Behind the closed door of his inner sanctum, he told us that he was sympathetic to our cause, but he couldn't vote his conscience. If he did, right-wingers in his district would send out Photoshopped postcards showing him cavorting with gay rights marchers in leather and chains. "And then I'll lose my seat, and y'all are goin' to get someone a whole lot worse in there," he told us.

If that visit was demoralizing, the mood outside in the hallway was downright hostile. Rumor had it that Representative Warren Chisum, one of the sponsors of the DOMA bill, had posted Texas State Troopers outside his door to ensure that no gays or gay sympathizers could come in. As we made our way down the polished granite corridors to see the Republican representative from Katy's parents' district, we didn't know what to expect. We were surprised to open the door on a crowded waiting room full of folks in their best Sunday clothes. Turns out, LGBT Lobby Day was also Brazoria County lobby day, and Rep. Dennis Bonnen's office was packed with locals who had bussed in to visit their elected officials' Austin offices.

With my big belly out in front, I led our small group through the crowd.

"We'd like to speak with the Representative about several bills that will negatively impact Texas families." The receptionist looked to be about the same age as the students in my sophomore writing class. She eyed my LGBT Lobby Day name tag.

"I'm sorry, Representative Bonnen is busy now, but I'll be glad to give him a message."

I launched into my talking points about how the proposed bills were bad for all Texans. The young woman looked somewhere between mortified and bored.

"I'm from Brazoria County," Katy interjected. "I grew up in Lake Jackson and lived there most of my life. I've always wanted to be a parent, and now my wife is carrying our baby that we've planned and prepared for together. Every night, I talk to her belly, tell him how much I love him. But if HB 916 passes, I won't be able to legally adopt him."

"Well, I will certainly tell the representative about your concerns," the woman said. She made a few cursory scratches on her yellow legal pad and then turned her eyes to the people waiting behind us. Dejected, we moved a few steps away to regroup. I looked around for an empty seat. It was exhausting, telling this story about our vulnerability in such a public way. And it didn't seem to be doing any good.

"Excuse me," a short man with dark hair and a notebook was standing at Katy's elbow. "I couldn't help overhearing your conversation. I'm a reporter from *The Brazosport Facts*, and I wondered if you'd be willing to be interviewed for a story about those bills you mentioned."

When she finished the interview, Katy called Donna to warn her that a story might appear in the *Facts*. Over the years, Donna had fed the local paper a steady stream of stories about the exploits of the Koonce family. The *Facts* had covered everything from Donna's triumph in the country club talent show to the Koonce's fortieth wedding anniversary to Big Phil's retirement from coaching. These were not little two-inch society column tidbits, either. On more than one occasion, the Koonce family had been the topic of two-page in-depth features that bore a striking resemblance to Donna's storytelling style. When I flipped through the family scrapbook, I gained a new respect for Donna's talents as a ghostwriter and public relations specialist.

But while the Koonce family was no stranger to local publicity, this latest article seemed to give Donna pause. "Are you sure you should be telling people your business?" she asked Katy.

"Just let Dad know what to expect, okay?" Katy sighed.

On the morning of April 6, Daddy Phil woke up around 7:00 and shuffled down the driveway to pick up the paper. Like a true diva, Donna habitually slept until 11 or even noon, so Phil usually ate breakfast and read the paper on his own. On this particular morning, however, he bypassed the kitchen table and made a beeline for Donna's bedroom, breaching her darkened sanctuary, and towering over her sleeping form.

"Donna, should Waylon have two mommies?" he asked in his deadpan Hank Hill drawl.

"What the hell?" Donna complained, peeking out from beneath her satin comforter.

"Should. Waylon. Have. Two. Mommies?" Big Phil repeated, pointing at the front-page headline.

It seemed to be the question of the year.

In a way, the newspaper did pose a relevant question. What should our son call us? It would be too confusing if we were both "Mommy." I knew some lesbian couples who used initials, like "Mom B" and "Mom J," but that seemed too formal. In my heart, I wanted to be called Mama, because that's what Katy's grandmother had been called—"Mama Babe" to be precise—although the Koonce family never pronounced it precisely. They contracted it into two Southern syllables that sounded like "Mam'babe." Mam'babe was small and angular and kind of severe looking, with a big nose and glasses, just like me. Yet her whole family adored her and called her by this romantic-sounding nickname that made her sound like a totally beloved babe.

It might seem presumptuous to appropriate a Koonce family name for myself, but Katy preferred to be called Mommy. She said that "Mommy" was the name she called when she skinned her knee or had a bad dream—like the time she got chicken pox and hallucinated a flock of angry snapping turtles outside her bedroom door.

Katy never flirted with "Maddy" or "Mapa" or any other name that bridged the gap between Mom and Dad. She knew that choosing to be called "Mommy" might tether her to the feminine end of the gender spectrum. But long ago, in her moments of childhood need, she had decided that a Mommy was the strongest thing she could be.

CHAPTER 10

The Sun Shines Out of His Behind

WHEN I WAS EIGHT-MONTHS pregnant, I watched a documentary about a lesbian couple whose baby was born without an anus.

"Hey," Katy whispered in the dark. "I'm not sure this is the best thing for you to be watching right now."

"I'm okay," I said, "Shhh!" I was perched on the edge of the seat, heavy belly balanced awkwardly on my thighs. I couldn't shift to a comfortable position until movie baby emerged from successful reconstructive surgery.

Later, I began to obsess on the possibility that our baby would be born with the same condition.

Katy tried in vain to assuage these fears. What was the likelihood, she asked, that another lesbian mom would have a baby with the same affliction that she'd seen in a movie? But worrying about a baby with no anus was about focusing my energies: instead of worrying a little bit about each of the thousands of things that could go wrong, I worried a lot about one particular thing.

When the nurse placed newborn baby Waylon on my chest, my mouth fell open. *I should close my mouth*, I thought. After eighteen hours in labor, a noise like chirping crickets was swelling in my ears, a wall of sound between thought and action.

Finally, a familiar voice distinguished itself from the din.

"Paige, he's beautiful. He's beautiful, Paige. Paige, he's beautiful." Katy's words were a trail of breadcrumbs; I followed them back to the present.

At that instant, a black lump slid across my belly. It was meconium, the baby's first shit. I looked at Katy.

"He has an anus!" Joy and relief and love washed over me in waves. He was beautiful! And healthy! I was so absorbed that I didn't see the puzzled looks on the nurses' faces.

"She saw a documentary, you know, about a baby who was born with no anus," Katy explained. "She was worried."

CHAPTER 11

Breast Is Best

WHEN WE CAME HOME from the hospital, my breasts had swollen to the size of grapefruits. Our friend Anne, mother of three, ordered me into the shower to relieve engorgement. Then she tucked me into clean sheets and placed Waylon against my side like a fragile football. As I struggled to connect his eager mouth to my nipple, Anne regaled me with stories of her own nursing days.

"I could shoot my husband with a stream of milk from ten feet away!" she crowed.

I doubted that I would be able to perform feats of milky athleticism. I am an angular person. I have a pointy nose, bony clavicles, and small, sharp breasts. I have never had the sense of confident abundance that I imagine to be the birthright of women with ample bosoms.

As the days passed, I nursed Waylon in every conceivable position at every conceivable time of day. A stack of books about breastfeeding towered at the side of the bed. When I wasn't gazing at his sweet, round moonface, I was balancing a book on my knee and studying the sensation of "let-down," when the baby's sucking stimulates the milk glands to release milk in a steady flow. *Is this it?* I asked, second-guessing every twinge and prickle.

At night, while Waylon slept beside us, I whispered secret fears. *It's not working. He's not getting enough.* Katy tried to provide comfort. "You're getting the hang of it," she said. "These are normal fears," she said. "If he were hungry, he'd let us know."

Indeed, Waylon's cries were insistent but moderate. He slept long hours for a newborn: five or six at a stretch. When he was awake, he had a habit of furrowing his brow and making his mouth into a little "o," like a tiny Zen master.

But when I looked at him, he seemed to be shrinking in tiny increments that were discernable only to me.

At his check-up, Waylon had lost three ounces. I confessed my concerns to the pediatrician and was personally escorted across the medical center to the breastfeeding specialist, as if I posed a flight risk.

The nurse escort kindly offered to carry my diaper bag. I trailed a few feet behind her, clutching Waylon to my chest and schlepping his infant carrier with my free arm. Every few steps, the carrier bumped against my leg, making my progress slow and lurching. When the nurse stopped to wait for me, I was humiliated and yet strangely relieved. Now that my incompetence was known to the world, help would surely follow.

The breastfeeding specialist was a white-haired hippie named Robbie. Her office was festooned with calico quilts and needlepoint aphorisms about the joys of motherhood. She assured me that lots of babies have trouble latching on and invited me to nurse Waylon on her homey couch. I obediently demonstrated a variety of holds. In each position, Waylon sucked enthusiastically at first and then lost interest.

Robbie connected my breasts to the hard plastic cups of a breast pump. She set the machine on low, then switched it to medium, frowning as she watched my milk dribble out. Finally, she asked permission to turn the wheezing machine all the way up. For the next 30 minutes, I mourned the former perkiness of my modest bosom. At last the machine came to a rest. I had produced a paltry four ounces of milk.

While Robbie outlined a detailed plan of frequent pumping between feedings, her helper fed Waylon a bottle of milk mixed with formula. I felt panicky, out-of-control. But this was no time to raise political objections about the medicalization of motherhood. Waylon sucked down the formula like a starving man and cried for more. After days of private calm, he was publicly ravenous.

My doctor prescribed pills to increase my milk supply. For some reason, they had to be ordered from an Internet pharmacy in New Zealand. I did not quibble, nor did I torture myself with Google searches of possible side effects. I ordered that shit, whatever it was, and I took it religiously.

As per Robbie's instructions, I pumped four times a day and nursed Waylon in between times. With the help of the mystery pills, I might, on a good day, produce eight ounces of milk in one sitting. Other moms had freezers *full* of eight ounce bottles. They swapped stories about leaking milk in meetings and rushing home from errands to relieve their aching breasts with blissful nursing. I nodded my head like I knew what they were talking about.

The new mother support group met at a member's house, a quaint little cottage that had grown a two-story addition on its rear end. The cheerful hostess greeted each woman in the foyer and ushered us down a long passageway into her tasteful, earth-toned living room.

I claimed a spot on the gleaming wood floor and arranged Waylon's toys on his play mat, hoping he wouldn't be crabby or restless. I knew that breast would be the pacifier *du jour*, but Waylon was increasingly accustomed to the bottle, which delivered milk quickly and reliably. At three months, he had become a picky, impatient nurser.

I hadn't yet decided whether to divulge my breastfeeding struggles, but I was encouraged by the mood of barely concealed desperation. Above the hummus and crackers, the air was heavy with expectation—as if, at any moment, the conversation would change from car seats and diapers to something very raw and poignant.

My sisters! I thought.

Then somebody opened the floodgates.

"*He* hands her back to me whenever she's fussy!"

"I left *him* alone with Bobby for three hours, and *he* watched television the whole time!"

"I just don't know how long I can go on like this—*he* acts like he doesn't know how to do anything."

"*He* sleeps through the night! While I'm awake with the baby!"

Husbands. The angst that I had sensed below the surface was about husbands! My internal sensor hovered between alienated and smug. I was disappointed to be outside of the conversation and yet glad not to share this particular problem. Katy called herself the "lesbian baby whisperer." She prided herself on the ability to soothe Waylon to sleep. She had changed her schedule to stay home with him in the mornings, so that I could go back to work part time. The fact that I was pumping and supplementing with formula meant that we could split the feedings. When Katy gave Waylon a bottle, he snuggled against her chest and gazed into her face. His fist clutched a lock of her long hair.

At Waylon's three-month check-up, a nurse quizzed me about Waylon's eating habits. "Still breastfeeding, right?"

I nodded vigorously, even as a lump formed in my throat.

"How many ounces a day, on average?"

I did the math out loud and quickly added, "I have to supplement with formula. I don't have enough milk." My voice sounded like a squeak.

The nurse made a note in Waylon's file. I wondered if she believed me, or if she was writing me off as a shirker.

"Well," she said, "breast is best, especially for the first six months. It builds his immune system."

"Yes," I said. "I know."

Originally I had planned to nurse for at least a year. Now the nurse's six month minimum loomed in my mind, an imaginary milestone that would save me from being a total fuck-up.

Then, at five and a half months, I got a cold. It wasn't a particularly terrible cold, but I felt so tired that I decided to skip the half hour of pumping just before bed. The next morning, when I woke up, my breasts weren't engorged. I nursed Waylon as usual, but since I still wasn't feeling good, I decided to skip the mid-morning pumping session in my office.

Freedom felt so great that I skipped lunchtime and mid-afternoon too. When I nursed Waylon that night, he was restless. I could tell that only a little milk was coming out, so I switched to a bottle. After months of feverish effort, I didn't have the energy to keep going.

Thus it was that breastfeeding went out, not with a bang or a whimper. The failure I feared had come to pass, and I was surprised to feel relieved. Occasional bouts of shame were balanced by moments of connection. We developed a ritual called "skin-on-skin," where Waylon would lie on my belly to cuddle. As I stroked his back in small circles, I could feel the good maternal hormones, the happiness of breathing as one, the touch that was helping my baby thrive and grow.

A month later, we went to visit our friend Lynzee, who had just had a baby. Although she's a generation younger than me, Lynzee is one of my favorite people in Lake Jackson. She's smart and funny and rocks a distinctive Latina hipster nerd fashion sense. She and her daughter, Laila, were living with Lynzee's mom in a two-bedroom apartment. Six weeks after Laila's birth, Lynzee had returned to her job as a cashier at Home Depot. I imagined the familiar orange apron draped across her chest. "How's breastfeeding going?" I asked.

As soon as the question was out of my mouth, I regretted it.

"Well..." Lynzee said, looking away, "breastfeeding's hard."

Surely there is someone who knows how to give a breastfeeding pep talk without shaming the recipient. I just haven't met her yet. In my experience, the laundry list of things-you-could-try can easily become a litany of reproach. For a moment, I felt tempted to launch into a white lady speech about infantile brain development and good antibodies. But I stopped myself.

"Yeah," I said, looking into her eyes. "I know."

CHAPTER 12

Fitted Shirt

AT NIGHT, WHEN WE finally got the baby to sleep, Katy would stand in front of the mirror, flattening her breasts with her hands. "I'd look pretty good, if it weren't for these," she said.

I was brushing my teeth, fighting for my share of mirror space. "Uh-huh." Spit. Rinse. Yawn. We had passed the part of new parenthood when people bring you casseroles and ask, "Are you getting any sleep?" with a sympathetic smile. At eighteen months, Waylon walked and talked and slept peacefully in his crib. He drank cow's milk and ate solid foods. But I still felt tired and drained. When I studied my reflection, I noticed dark circles, dull skin and limp, straggly hair.

One night, when Katy was bemoaning her silhouette-spoiling breasts, I mentioned that the holidays were coming. "Why don't you just do it? Schedule the surgery," I said, pulling my nightgown over my head. "I'll be off work when the semester ends. I can take care of you."

By the time I walked the two steps from the bathroom to the bedroom, Katy was already on Transter.com, looking at pictures of surgically reconstructed man chests. "I really like what Dr. Rafael is doing with pecs," she said, holding her laptop so I could see.

By age thirteen, it was clear that Katy had inherited her mother's legendary rack. And since she refused to set foot in the lingerie department, Katy was at the mercy of her mother's taste in bras. Thus, throughout the low-slung seventies, Katy was forced to sport Jayne Mansfield-style

76

bras that launched her boobs up and out, like minor planets orbiting her chin.

It was not a style that complemented a softball uniform. Or a basketball uniform. Or any of the other sporty ensembles that might otherwise have offered androgynous refuge for a budding butch. In the context of Katy's broad shoulders and chiseled jaw line, the bullet bras made femininity seem like awkward and unfortunate drag.

Throughout her teen years, Katy's parents pestered her to watch her weight. Looking back at old pictures, it's clear that Katy was a dedicated athlete who played multiple sports. Focusing on weight was her family's way of expressing discomfort with physical difference. They couldn't very well tell her to stop moving and looking like a linebacker with boobs; they had no language for gender nonconformity. They might have known words like "butch" or "dyke," but their implications would have been unspeakable. Weight became the focal point for the desire to fix a body that refused to be fully feminine.

Her parents, especially her mother, would live to regret it. When Katy was nineteen, she moved to Hollywood. She stopped wearing bullet bras and began wearing tight long-sleeved leotards under her clothes. At first she favored the leotards because they flattened her chest. Later she needed the leotards to cover her track marks.

When Katy came home to Texas for a visit, her parents were ecstatic. "Finally," Donna wrote in the family photo album, "a size 6!" It's easy to understand how she was beguiled. In photographs from that era, Katy looks skinny, even a bit gaunt. But she also looks comfortable in her body, more congruent, confident, and sexy. Katy told her parents that she had discovered a remarkable new diet medicine. In fact, she had discovered a powerful means to androgenize her body: crystal meth.

When she was homeless, hungry, living in her car and cheap motels, her mother came to fetch her from Hollywood. Even then, Katy wasn't ready to give up on speed and the relief it afforded from dysphoria. She clung to it until she realized that the drugs had changed more than her body—she had become a person whom she did not like or respect—and then she quit.

By that time, Katy's parents had changed too. Katy had come out as a lesbian when she moved to Hollywood, and her family had accepted the news with love and grace.

"You know," her dad said one day, in his deadpan East Texas drawl, "that k.d. lang is a lezben." Now retired, the old coach was less attached to having a particular kind of daughter and was simply glad that she had survived. Thus, when Katy gained back weight and boobs, she was able to convince her parents to pay for a partial breast reduction. Donna even accompanied Katy to nearby Galveston to meet the plastic surgeon, Dr. Ted Huang.

"She'd just like a nice B cup," Donna informed the doctor, making a suggestive cupping gesture with her hand.

"Mom! I want to be flat," Katy corrected. "I want people to look at me and say 'that girl is *so* flat!'"

Katy had no idea that Dr. Huang was affiliated with the Rosenberg Clinic, one of the oldest gender clinics in the South. She'd never heard of genderqueer people or trans men or the transgender community. She had no idea that there were other people who felt the way she did.

Apparently, Dr. Huang did not feel compelled to enlighten her on these points. But he did remove eight pounds of breast tissue from Katy's chest. The breast reduction didn't leave her totally flat, and it didn't resolve her feelings of gender dysphoria, but it did make living in her body a lot more bearable.

As usual, we made the decision first and asked questions later. How much would it cost? How would we pay? Most importantly, what would the baby say?

At eighteen months, Waylon mostly said nouns: *Mama, Mommy, doggie.* And he had commands: *More. Ba-ba.* And *up-up,* which meant "I want to be picked up."

"Mommy's chest is going to be different," I said. We were lying in bed while Waylon enjoyed his morning bottle of milk. "But Mommy will still love you just the same."

Waylon's big blue eyes watched me over his bottle. I wondered how much he even noticed Katy's breasts. She hadn't nursed him, but she fed and bathed and diapered and dressed him. She built towers of blocks and watched Elmo and cuddled until lunchtime, when she dropped him off at day care.

She hadn't nursed him, but she did dispense metaphorical milk. As a therapist, Katy worked from a psychoanalytic theory called "object relations," which views a baby's relationship to the mother's breast as the crucible of all future relationships.

Initially, so the theory goes, the baby experiences a present, abundant breast as "good breast." Baby loves good breast. But an absent or empty breast—when baby is crying and no one picks it up, for example—is "bad breast." Baby hates bad breast and is flooded with aggressive, destructive feelings. Eventually, with fairly consistent care, the child comes to understand that good breast and bad breast are one and the same, that the mother is a separate person, with separate needs. When that doesn't happen, there's a tendency to split other people into good or bad, to careen between love and hate.

In this school of thinking, the therapist becomes an emotional stand-in for the maternal breast. Through consistency and empathy, Katy hoped to help people move beyond early, disorganizing experiences of loss and want. Now, on the verge of surgery, Katy worried how her clients would react, and whether they could maintain a connection to a morphing breast.

We talked about how the surgery would affect everyone else, but we didn't devote much time talking about the surgery's potential impact on our relationship. The obvious question—*Why now, when Waylon is still*

a baby?—went unuttered. Of course, Katy wouldn't have been inclined to introduce obstacles. Gender dysphoria was the thorn in her side, and surgery represented sweet relief. I felt the promise of relief too. When we made love, Katy's breasts were a minefield. If I touched them, even by accident, I could feel her body stiffen and her mind grow distant.

Loving her as I did, I couldn't help wanting her to feel more at home in her body. And besides, I'd always known that chest surgery was on the horizon, ever since I'd first spotted her wearing her prosthetic man chest in Raunchy Reckless and the Amazons. I could hardly be surprised that she jumped at the opportunity once I gave the green light. But that still begs the question: Why did I propose the time myself, especially when I was still feeling so spent and exhausted by the demands of motherhood?

Perhaps I was eager for change precisely because of the way that parenting was transforming my identity. My days were a constant cycle of feeding, diapering and coaxing Waylon into sleep. I barely had time to write in my journal, much less work on my 'zine. During the week, I went to my job at the university, which involved increasing amounts of responsibility. I had a full-time assistant now, plus a quarter-time teaching appointment and a rotating cast of graduate assistants. However, as a non-faculty staff person, I was afforded limited recognition for my work. Every program that I developed had to have a faculty figurehead who lent legitimacy to my efforts and received credit for successes that my team and I created. At the end of a grueling day at work, I rushed to the daycare to pick up Waylon and returned to the demands of feeding and diapering and story time and sleep.

On weekends, we shuttled Waylon to baby music class and took him on long walks in his stroller. We still attended anti-war marches and queer political protests, but we had to schedule our participation around his nap schedule. In the evenings, we hurried home to relieve the babysitter when everyone else stayed out into the wee hours. When *The L Word* debuted on television, a dedicated group of friends came to our house to make fun of the Hollywood depiction of lesbian lives. Ironically, that

Sunday night ritual was becoming the most reliable moment of queer community in our week.

When I'd met and fallen in love with Katy, I'd been determined to live a bigger, bolder life, beyond the strictures of what people expected of me. Now work and parenthood were boxing me in again. Perhaps supporting Katy through her surgery would offer a way out. If the daily demands of parenthood were mundane and culturally determined, the demands of making a trans family seemed like exciting, uncharted territory. If my political participation felt constrained, transition was a process in which the personal acts were imbued with political significance. If my professional life offered little in the way of distinction or recognition, being a supportive partner seemed to offer a chance to shine.

In the trans world, SOFFA is an acronym for Significant Others Family Friends and Allies. I had seen several documentaries where significant others complained about the narcissism and self-involvement of the transitioning partner. I thought the whole narcissistic trans partner narrative was transphobic, and I was determined that the same bitterness would not befall me. I would be patient. I would be self-sacrificing. I would care for Katy with unflagging compassion and political commitment. If supporting someone else was an unlikely way to define my identity, I refused to reckon with that contradiction. I would be the perfect sofa.

For years, Katy had favored oversized men's shirts with dragons or pin-up girls or flaming guitars. Gaudy and baggy, they distracted the eye and disguised her breasts. As the surgery grew near, she began to buy tight, black fitted shirts. Pin stripe shirts that hugged the pecs. Gay boy shirts that emphasized abs. She tucked these new shirts in her suitcase and planned to start wearing them as soon as she emerged from surgery.

I packed my overnight bag with nail polish, hair color, and a clay facemask. This would be the first time that Katy and I were both away from Waylon overnight. My sister Kristen—Waylon's doting and enthusiastic auntie—was coming to stay with him, and I planned to take full advantage of the respite. While Katy recovered from surgery, I would cleanse my pores, fix my roots and give myself a pedicure.

Dr. Rafael's office is located in Plano, an aptly named suburb of the sprawling Dallas-Fort Worth metroplex. On a chilly fall morning, we navigated past big box stores and subdivisions, arriving at the surgery center well before sunrise. I had expected a plastic surgeon's office to be glamorous, but the surgery waiting room was a cramped space with fluorescent lights, beat-up black leather couches and outdated magazines.

We sat in nervous silence until a friendly nurse summoned us to the pre-surgical area. Katy donned a hospital gown while I stuffed her clothes in a plastic bag. She handed me her wedding ring and unscrewed the metal barbell from her tongue. Then Dr. Raphael entered the room and asked Katy to sit on the side of the bed with the gown around her waist.

The surgeon looked at Katy's chest appraisingly, his marker hovering over the center of each breast. I felt protective, because Katy is a very modest person, but she didn't seem to mind. She was too engrossed in discussing the details of her future nipples, which would be flatter and further apart. She didn't even flinch when the doctor examined the side-boob area beneath her armpits. In order to create a more masculine physique, the doctor planned to liposuction this telltale bit of feminine fat.

When the doctor left the room, the recovery nurse came in to introduce herself. "What did you bring to wear after the surgery?"

I rummaged in Katy's bag and held up a fitted shirt from H+M. "How's this?"

The nurse looked amused. "She's going to have drains on each side. She'll need something roomy, something you can open and close easily."

Katy looked distraught.

"Don't worry," I said, "I'll figure it out."

A few minutes later, the surgery nurse arrived. I pressed my cheekbone hard into Katy's cheek, so she would feel my touch as long as she was still conscious.

"I love you," I said. "And I'm so happy for you."

After the gurney disappeared down the long hallway, I walked to the car and sat in the dark, gathering my thoughts. Then I drove to the 24-hour Wal-Mart, where I found an extra large men's hoodie. It wasn't what she wanted, but—at 6 a.m. in Plano, Texas—it was the best I could do.

Back in the waiting room, I took off my coat, which had been missing a button for months. Less than a hundred feet away, the doctor was sewing Katy's nipples back on. I found the needle and thread that I'd tucked in my purse and patted my pockets for the missing button. As I pulled the long thread through the thick wool fabric, I pictured myself serene and domestic, the Betsy Ross of SOFFAs.

A couple of hours later, another nurse called my name. I found Katy in a makeshift recovery room—a row of gurneys with curtains between them. She was groggy, barely conscious and in pain.

"You made it!" I said. "You survived!"

"It hurts," she groaned.

The friendly pre-op nurse had been replaced by the brusque recovery nurse with a frowning, chiseled face. She handed Katy a graham cracker and a juice box. She handed me a stack of instructions, which she proceeded to read at breakneck speed.

"You need to fill these prescriptions immediately. Give her this one every eight hours and this one every four hours as needed. Sign here."

I initialed the first of many checklists.

"These bandages should not be changed until she meets with the doctor. If you notice excessive bleeding or swelling, call this number immediately. Sign here."

"These are her drains," she said, undoing Katy's gown. Below each armpit, the bandages opened to admit a long, clear plastic tube full of red and yellow liquid. "They need to be cleared every half hour while she's awake, like this." Holding the tube at the top with one hand, she squeezed downward with the other, milking it into a plastic container that looked like a transparent grenade.

"Every time you clear the drains, you need to record the amount of fluid here." She flipped to a chart in the stack of instructions.

"It's very important to be precise, so that the doctor can monitor the swelling."

She pulled the grenade off the end of the tube and emptied its contents into a small plastic measuring cup. A thick, white, fibrous substance clung to the mouth of the container, and she tapped it against the side of the cup. "You may see some tissue in there, that's normal."

Suddenly, the chair at Katy's bedside looked very inviting. Would it be so wrong to rest for a moment with my head between my knees? No, Katy was awake and groaning softly at my elbow, I needed to stay strong.

"Help me get her pants on," the nurse said. "Then I'll finish dressing her while you bring the car around."

Wait. What? The car? Already? I knew this was day surgery, but I expected a little more buffer between surgery and flying solo.

The nurse sat Katy up and swung her legs around the side of the bed. Katy looked like she was about to spew graham crackers across the recovery room. I wanted to beg the nurse for more instruction, more recovery time, but she was moving quickly, inexorably. Before I could regain composure, she was pulling Katy's pants up over her hips. Katy swayed on her feet. I ran to fetch the car.

Twenty minutes later, we pulled up to Economy Suites. I guided Katy through the dank lobby, past the vending machine offering microwave meals, and into our gloomy room. I tucked her between scratchy sheets and fed her a pain pill from the pharmacy bag. She slipped mercifully into sleep.

Economy Suites was one of two extended-stay hotels recommended by Dr. Rafael's office. I knew that some people had to stay several nights for recovery, and the cost of five nights in a hotel could really add up. But still. It seemed cruel to send trans folks here, to this seedy motel full of lonely men eating chili out of microwave-safe cans. It was not the place you'd want to wake up on the first day of the rest of your life.

I opened the curtains and thought longingly of the Sheraton I'd seen on the edge of town, its gleaming white bathroom so conducive to pedicures and facials. I lounged on the bed, flipped through all six channels, and read an advertisement for Domino's Pizza on the back of my key card. I removed the skeezy polyester bedspread and washed my hands. It was time to empty Katy's drains.

When we returned home the next day, Katy slept and watched *Teletubbies* with Waylon. Every few hours, I cleared the drains and helped wrap her chest with compression bandages. The swelling had gone down, but not enough. She still couldn't fit into the shirts of her dreams.

I knew she was frustrated. I felt sorry for her, but not as sorry as I felt for myself, because the doctor had forbidden Katy to lift anything heavy for six weeks. In the morning, I carried Waylon down the stairs and installed him in the high chair. When he was wet, I lifted him onto the changing table. If we left the house, I put him in the car seat or the stroller. At night, I lowered him into the tub and settled him in the crib.

My sister had generously stayed in town to help with Waylon. However, there are times in every marriage when it's best not to have a witness. This is especially true when your sister is a sociologist who studies gender and inequality. Instead of feeling relieved to have another set of hands, I worried how my parental responsibilities must look from her point of view. I imagined her silently adding up the hours of my second shift and shaking her head disapprovingly.

Waylon was having a hard time too, because Katy couldn't pick him up. When she stood to walk across the room, he would present himself to her, "Up! Up!" with arms outstretched. "I can't pick you up right now," Katy said, looking guilty. "Come sit with me." She returned to the couch and patted the spot next to her. Waylon looked confused, then crestfallen. "Up-up?" It had always worked before.

Meanwhile, the more Katy's wounds healed, the more they itched. To reduce scarring, Dr. Rafael had closed the incisions with heavy silk tape that looked like grosgrain ribbon across her chest. We were supposed to leave the tape in place until it fell off on its own, so Katy scratched in tiny, careful strokes around the edges, desperate for relief but afraid to disturb the incisions. Sometimes, after I re-wrapped her double layer of extra-wide ace bandages, she'd grab a bamboo back scratcher and try to soothe herself with symbolic scratching above and below the bandage.

Finally, after a week of lying around like a miserable, trussed-up turkey, Katy got up from the couch, washed, and put on clean clothes. Her pain was receding, and I felt like I could see the light at the end of the tunnel. I imagined myself sitting at a café, alone, reading a book. I was ecstatic at the prospect of a few hours with no baby to carry, no meals to fix, no drains to empty—a blissful, well-deserved reward for all the hard days of nursing and child care.

"Babe," Katy said, "I think I'll just run out to the mall and buy some shirts that fit."

My throat tightened and I felt like I was going to cry. My sister was sitting on the floor, playing with Waylon. I thought I saw her purse her lips.

"Oh," I said in a small, cramped voice. "I was hoping to have a break."

"I know!" Katy said, as if she'd just had a stroke of inspiration. "Why don't we go to the mall together? You can help me pick out shirts!"

In that moment, I felt I had made a terrible mistake. I had joined my life to a terrible narcissist with no regard for my needs, no sympathy for my suffering. The rich tapestry of our lives together unraveled to a single moment in time, and I plunged from disappointment to anger to despair. My needs had never been met. I was sure they would never, ever be met again.

In every long-term relationship, people have to manage conflicting needs. It gets messy, and it requires unbelievable reserves of empathy and trust. You have to be able to hold on to past experiences of abundance, and you have to believe that your turn will come again. But I was running on empty. My reserves of faith and empathy were dangerously low. And Katy's needs were urgent and epic and undeniable. I mean, what was I supposed to say? *Sorry, I can't help you realize your life-long dream of feeling comfortable in your body because I need to get a pedicure right now?*

So I went with Katy to buy shirts. And I simmered.

Part II

Katy at around seven

Paige models a groovy
seventies pantsuit

Paige in a maxi-dress inspired by the Sunshine Family

Katy performs as Koonce the Vulgar Viking in
Raunchy Reckless and the Amazons.

Paige as a go-go dancer at Gaby and Mo's.

Brian performs with one of his bands in the eighties.

Brian and Katy back in the day: "Whoa, that dude looks like me."

Paige and Katy on their wedding day.

Aerial view: Donna grabs the mic from Gretchen.

CHAPTER 13

Interferon Interrupts

THROUGHOUT MY STORY, I'VE taken it upon myself to characterize Katy's interior states, but her pain has eluded me. Perhaps it's because I can't really know what it's like, or perhaps it's because it makes me feel powerless. But most likely it's because the pain was so ordinary and pervasive that it never quite coalesced into a narratable event. Think of it as the street noise in the soundtrack of our story. Occasionally the pitch would rise and the volume would swell until it drowned out everything else, but most of the time it remained at a dull roar.

Katy's paternal grandfather died of complications related to rheumatoid arthritis, an autoimmune disease that causes the immune system to attack the membranes surrounding the joints. Katy likely shared his genetic predisposition, but it didn't manifest until her thirties, when she underwent two rounds of treatment with interferon—a powerful antiviral drug used to treat hepatitis C. The interferon didn't clear the hep C, but it did kick Katy's immune system into high gear. By the time we got together, her efforts to cure hepatitis had taken a backseat to coping with the daily indignities of rheumatoid arthritis.

Then Waylon was born, and everything changed. Katy wanted to live to see her baby grow up. And if she was going to stick around for the long haul, she knew she needed to make living in her body more bearable. Chest surgery was the obvious first step. And then, while her chest was still shrouded in surgical bandages, Katy's liver doctor mentioned a promising new treatment for hepatitis C: a long-acting form of interferon with whimsical brand name "Pegasys." When paired with another drug called ribavirin, Pegasys (or peginterferon alfa-2a) granted a new lease on life to roughly 45 percent of people with Katy's strain of the virus. For someone like Katy, who had never responded to interferon before, the odds were not quite as good. It was a long shot, but it might be the only shot she had. If she wanted to vanquish the deadly virus, she would have to take another round of the drug that had triggered her arthritis.

Before Waylon was born, Katy probably would have said no. But these days we didn't joke about her early demise. Instead of fantasizing about a booze cruise as her last hurrah, Katy measured her lifespan in terms of Waylon's future. If she died in her sixties, Waylon would be in his twenties, far too young to lose a parent. If she developed cirrhosis or liver cancer—common outcomes for untreated hep C—her illness would leave lasting scars on his young psyche.

Ultimately, the decision was Katy's alone. Only she knew how harrowing the previous treatment had been, and only she knew if she could face it again. I said I would support her either way, but I breathed a big sigh of relief when she decided to try. I knew the earlier treatment had been awful. I'd heard stories about the pain and fatigue that left her unable to perform even the simplest tasks. But I clung to the hope that everything would be different this time. Before she had been alone, and the whole experience had been frightening and overwhelming. But now she had me and Waylon—two very good reasons to get well.

Katy came home from her next doctor's appointment with a hefty book of patient information for pegylated interferon. After we put Waylon to bed that night, I settled down on the couch to read up on what to expect. Soon I was drowning in a sea of potential side effects: anemia, anorexia, fatigue. Suicidal thoughts, shortness of breath, confusion, cold chills. Heart attack, pneumonia, thyroid failure. Relapse of drug abuse. Stroke. Loss of vision, loss of hair, joint pain, fever, and malaise. Clearly, it would have been easier to list the one or two medical conditions that were *not* possible side effects. I put the book on the shelf.

In the past, my neurotic pessimism had served its purposes. (If I imagined that my baby would be born with no anus, I could be pleasantly surprised when he pooped on my chest.) But now the worst-case scenario was simply too bleak. My brain refused to process what I'd read in the patient manual. Instead of anticipating symptoms, I took refuge in magical thinking. I would single-handedly stave off side effects! Like a modern-day Clara Barton, I would lay cool compresses on Katy's fevered brow. I would plump her pillows and massage her aching joints. I would soothe her nausea with soda crackers and bolster her with bowls of chicken soup. I was certain that love and patience would make all the difference.

CHAPTER 14

Dead Frog

IN A MATTER OF weeks, my strong, vivacious spouse became a ghost who spent most of her time dozing in front of the television. In the morning, she had to brace her back against the railing and sidestep down the stairs. Simple tasks, like making breakfast, exhausted her. Once upon a time, she'd been the extrovert who pulled me out into the world, but now I had to provide the motivation and energy for all outings. Once I'd looked forward to weekends as family time, but now weekends were particularly lonely, because Katy did her interferon shot on Thursday night and then spent the next few days riding out the immediate symptoms—nausea, body aches, cold sweats, and fatigue.

I spent weekend mornings pushing Waylon around the neighborhood in his stroller, because it allowed us to get out of the house without getting too far away from Katy if she needed us. I tried to keep up my end of the conversation—"Look, a kitty cat! Let's count how many cats we see on our walk today!"—but sometimes my mind wandered to the vision of the happy strolling trio that Katy had conjured back when she was wooing me.

"Oh look, a frog!" I said absently. As soon as the words were out of my mind, I regretted them. It was, indeed, a frog. But it was dead.

"What's wrong with the frog, Mama?"

"Oh, sweetie," I said, willing myself back into the present. "It's really sad, but the frog got squished by a car."

"Will it get better?"

"No, it can't get better. The frog isn't alive any more. Goodbye, Frog. Bye-bye."

"Bye-bye, Frog!"

I steered the stroller away from the scene and hoped it would soon be forgotten, but Waylon regurgitated the story for weeks, his baby brain working hard to internalize the boundary between life and death.

"We saw a frog in the road?"

"Yes."

"It was dead."

"That's right."

"A car can squish you in a heartbeat." This was the warning he had heard a hundred times from his parents. Now, issuing from his cherub lips, the familiar words were stripped of custom and metaphor. The reality of death felt stark and new.

CHAPTER 15

Not a Poster Family

WAYLON'S FIRST ENCOUNTER WITH death occurred shortly before his second birthday. In the ensuing hubbub of party balloons and presents, the smushed frog was temporarily forgotten. Kids from pre-school ran wild in the backyard, licking frosting from cupcakes and then abandoning them in the bushes. Donna Koonce made a rare visit to Austin—ostensibly to celebrate her grandson's birthday, but also to check on the health of her daughter. The two presided over the party from canvas camp chairs on the back porch—Donna smoking her signature Carlton 120s, Katy looking tired and pale, but happy.

A week later, on May 21, 2005, the Texas state senate passed a proposed amendment banning same-sex marriage and civil unions. Since the state had already banned same-sex unions in the previous session, this effort to amend the constitution was a legislative middle finger in the face of gay and bisexual Texans: *In case you've forgotten, you're not welcome here, queers.* And this episode of legislative gay bashing wouldn't end when the legislature adjourned at the end of May, because Texas law requires constitutional amendments to be ratified by a popular vote. Come November, Proposition 2 would be the perfect occasion to rally the conservative base during an off-year election.

Thus, on a Sunday afternoon in early June, I found a babysitter for Waylon and cajoled Katy to a meeting of the grassroots opposition. It was across town, at the home of a lesbian couple that we vaguely knew. We arrived late, and the overstuffed couches in the high-ceilinged great room were already crowded with earnest political bodies. I scanned the room for a familiar face. None of our close friends were there. Either same-sex marriage wasn't their issue, or else they thought that the passage of Prop 2 was a foregone conclusion—or both.

I was hesitant to dive in, but I was aware of Katy standing woozy and winded at my side. I took her arm and led her through the crowd, finally locating an empty stool at the granite-topped kitchen island in the back.

At the front of the room stood a round-faced man with graying hair and a rumpled polo shirt. He looked like a youngish grandpa, but he spoke in the world-weary tones of a political insider. It was Glen Maxey, our former state rep, and the first openly gay man to be elected to the Texas legislature. He was explaining that voter turnout in Texas was pitifully low.

"Well, I think people will turn out to vote for fairness," said a grey-haired woman in Birkenstocks. "Gay marriage is about fairness,"

Maxey shook his head. "The data tells us that abstract concepts like 'fairness' and 'justice' don't resonate with voters," he said emphatically.

Many people around the room looked like they'd received a blow, and Maxey seemed to take a certain pleasure in bursting their bubbles. "We have to appeal to their values, the things that they care about, like keeping government out of people's lives."

"That's right," said a soft butch with a West Texas accent. "They don't want the government to take away their guns, and they don't want the government nosing around in their bedroom either."

The discussion of good old-fashioned Texas values quickly veered into enthusiastic endorsement of patriotic ideals, with several audience members averring that gay people paid taxes and served their country "just like everyone else."

I thought about the thousands of civilians who had died since the U.S. had invaded Iraq. I wasn't about to pay lip service to American values, as if everything in the nation would be just ducky once gay people had the right to marry. *What the hell am I doing here?* I asked myself. But then my mind flitted to the flimsy power of attorney that we'd printed off the Internet when Katy started her treatment. Would it stand up in court? Would it guarantee that I could stay with Katy if she ended up in the hospital? I imagined myself pacing a waiting room while she languished behind a locked door that said "family only." These fears squeezed my heart with icy fingers and reminded me what was at stake.

"I think the idea of 'family' will certainly resonate with voters," said a gay dad in khakis and a sparkling white oxford shirt. "We just need to introduce them to our beautiful families."

"Yesssss," Maxey said carefully. "We will need a few carefully selected spokespeople, both gay and straight."

I cast a sidelong glance at Katy. She was blotting her pale, sweaty face with a bandanna. It didn't take a political strategist to predict that a queer family with one ailing, tattooed, gender-ambiguous parent would not be among the "carefully selected" spokesfamilies. I felt resentment rising in my chest. For a few seconds, I started to hate all these respectable-looking people with their healthy families.

I reeled myself in. *At least these people are here. At least they're doing something to fight back.* I couldn't stand the thought of remaining passive while conservative politicians ground us into the dirt under their pointy-toed boots. To preserve my dignity—and maybe even my sanity—I knew I had to fight back. But I also knew that my resources were limited. With a toddler, a full-time job and a sick spouse, I couldn't make an impact on my own. I had to throw my lot in with someone else.

By the time my attention returned to the moment, the group was hammering out a slogan ("No Nonsense in November") and a strategy (mobilize progressive faith communities). If the slogan was calculated to offend no one, it also seemed unlikely to enlighten or explain much either. As for the strategy—well, churches had nurseries and playgrounds where Waylon could play. They also had pews where Katy could rest, and maybe even a committee to bring casseroles to the sick. Mobilizing in progressive faith communities seemed like it might be about my speed.

When we returned home from the meeting, Katy fell into bed. It was 90 degrees outside, but her hands were cold as ice.

"Babe, you have to call the doctor tomorrow."

"I know," she said wearily.

The doctor sent her to get blood drawn, and we soon learned that Katy had developed anemia. That's why she was so pale and cold and clammy all the time.

Undeterred, the doctor prescribed weekly injections of Procrit, which treats anemia by increasing red blood cells. Like interferon, Procrit had to be injected into subcutaneous fat. Katy had inherited her mother's bony ass and skinny thighs, so she had to inject both medicines into the fat on her belly. Bruises bloomed in various stages of purple and green and yellow across her vulnerable middle. Each time I caught a glimpse of her battered flesh, a jolt of fear pushed my body into fight or flight mode. I had to do something to protect the people I loved.

CHAPTER 16

The Space at the Side of the Bed

At 5 a.m. the next Saturday morning, I made the mistake of rolling over in my sleep. Katy had been lying awake, wracked with pain, but her hands weren't working and she couldn't get to her pain meds. She'd been waiting for some sign of life from me, and now was her chance. "Babe, are you awake?"

"I am now."

"My hands are hurting real bad. I need you to get my meds for me."

Now that the interferon had been in her system for several weeks, Katy's arthritis flared with a vengeance. Often she woke up moaning in pain because her elbows or shoulders had gotten locked in place. She had to suck in her breath, tense her body and then force the joint to move with a sickening crack.

On this particular morning, I was groggy and grumpy. I rolled out of bed, practically stomped to the dresser and fished three pills out of a large bottle of Vicodin. Without speaking a word, I slipped them onto Katy's tongue and then held the water glass to her lips. I was tired, so deeply, bone-numbingly tired, and I desperately wanted to get back to sleep. I flopped back in the bed and pulled the blanket over my head.

Just as I was drifting off again, I heard Waylon calling from the next room—softly at first and then more and more insistently. I tried to ignore it, hoping against hope that the pain meds had kicked in and Katy would bounce out of bed.

"Babe," she said, in her pitiful, sickly voice, "Waylon's calling you."

I flipped off the covers and shuffled into Waylon's room, which was painted like a red-and-yellow striped circus tent. He was leaning against the bars of his crib, arms outstretched.

"Mama," he said with a smile, "I want milk." I hefted him over the bars and onto my hip. At two, he was too big to still be sleeping in a crib. A more physically adventurous child would have climbed out on his own, but Waylon preferred to be waited upon.

I carried him downstairs and poured a large sippy cup full of cow milk. Even though he'd been off the bottle for a while, he was still in the habit of drinking milk every morning, and sometimes he'd fall asleep again after he finished. Back upstairs, I settled him into the bed between Katy and me. I stroked his long, blonde hair while he gulped his morning snack. Eventually, I saw his lids start to flicker. I closed my eyes, hoping he'd mirror me. In minutes, I heard the sippy cup fall to his side. I relaxed and sank back into sleep.

In my dream, I was standing at the chalkboard in front of my students with a wet, sloppy sensation in my lower half. Something was wrong with my clothes. I looked down and saw blood flowing down my leg and onto the shiny white tile. *Disaster!* I wrenched myself awake, vaguely aware of physical discomfort, but it took me a few minutes to recognize the pain in my lower back and the wetness on my thighs as signs that my period had started in real life. I hoisted myself out of bed and walked, very carefully, to the bathroom.

When I returned, Katy and Waylon were still asleep. I popped a couple of Advil. Cramps were coming hard and fast, and I prayed that both of my charges would stay asleep. I slid into bed and pulled my knees up to my chest, hoping to relieve the spasms in my lower back.

"No Grady, that's my toy!" I must have drifted off again, because I was awakened by Waylon's one-sided conversation. He was babbling to himself, rehearsing the little conflict-resolution scripts that he'd learned in preschool. I thought ruefully of the time before chest surgery and interferon, when Katy and I had split up the weekend mornings so that each of us got one day per weekend to sleep late. Now I was lucky if she got up from bed or couch all day. I turned over to look at her. She was awake. We were all awake.

"My elbows hurt so bad last night," she said. "That was brutal." I knew it wasn't worth mentioning my cramps.

I gathered Waylon up and walked him downstairs, leaving Katy to sleep. I made coffee and watched Waylon play with his toy trains, trying to muster enthusiasm for the engines' endless trips around the track. I felt lonely and abandoned. I knew I should be mad at the disease, but that was too abstract. I felt mad at Katy, and that made me feel like a terrible person.

CHAPTER 17

Church Ladies

ON A SUNDAY MORNING in late June, I hurried down the driveway and shoved the diaper bag in the backseat of our car. Katy and Waylon straggled behind me. After she buckled Waylon into his car seat, Katy dropped into the driver's seat with an exhausted sigh. It takes twice as long to get ready to go somewhere when you have a toddler. You have to pack diapers and snacks and spare clothes. You've got to figure out when they napped last and what they will play with when you arrive. Now, with Katy sick, it took our family three times as long to get ready. I had to let her sleep until the last possible moment, then coax her into wakefulness. If she hadn't taken her pills, then she might have to eat something, and once she was dressed, I never knew when she might feel dizzy or nauseous and have to lie down again.

We were headed to the Unitarian Universalist church. I hadn't been to any church in more than fifteen years, but I knew the UUs by reputation: intellectual, progressive, and practically secular. I figured the least I could do to fight Prop 2 would be to rub shoulders with a bunch of folks who were probably itching to vote against the amendment anyway. Besides, I was tired of piloting the stroller around the neighborhood without Katy at my side. Despite her frail health, I knew that my New Agey spouse would jump out of bed if I showed even the slightest interest in something spiritual.

At ten past nine, Katy pulled our station wagon into the crowded church parking lot. A few stragglers were making their way from the overflow parking in the grassy lot next door. They looked more like museum docents and junior high school principals than the long-haired Austin liberals I'd imagined. My heart skipped a beat.

I'd been raised Catholic, but my mother had been raised by Mormon parents who left the Latter Day Saints church when she was twelve. As the daughter of apostates, she had inherited a hearty skepticism about church authority, which she struggled to keep under wraps after marrying my dad. When I was old enough to make my first confession, she helped me memorize the difference between mortal and venial sins—but she also whispered in my ear that there was no fire and brimstone for mortal sinners, no hell where human beings were cut off from God's grace. When the nuns taught me that the pasty communion wafers were the literal body of Christ, my mother subtly questioned the doctrine of transubstantiation, slyly suggesting that "some people" understood the Eucharist as a symbol.

Mom's careful questions and whispered asides could have turned me into a good Protestant, but I was confused by the fact that we continued to attend mass, week after week, when neither she nor my father ever spoke with real conviction about their Catholic faith. As a teenager, I concluded that all religion was an empty shell, a series of rote actions people performed because they thought they should.

My parents didn't make a fuss when I refused to be confirmed, and I had always believed that I didn't have much religious baggage. Now, as sweat pooled in the sleeves of my pink sundress, I was beginning to wonder if I'd underestimated the half-life of my Catholic girlhood. I grabbed the diaper bag from the backseat and rummaged around for a wipe to remove the leftover carrots from Waylon's lower lip. I couldn't shake the feeling that someone was going to jump out from behind a car and denounce us as sinners.

I must have looked nervous, because Katy took my hand as we turned toward the church. Instead of feeling comforted, I was beset by a wave of guilt. In all my insistence that we get out of the house and DO something, in all my ruminations on my own religious history, I hadn't stopped to consider how comfortable church would be for her as a genderqueer person. Would people stare at her? Would they call her "brother" and then get flustered when they heard her feminine voice? Would small children cling to their parents' knees and ask in loud voices whether she was a girl or a boy?

"Are you really okay with this?" I asked as we approached the church.

"Yeah," she smiled at me. "I'm good."

I took a deep breath, pushed through the heavy wooden door, and was accosted by a wave of familiar institutional smells: dusty chalkboards, burnt coffee, and construction paper. Strains of singing wafted into the empty lobby. A tall woman with grey, curly hair and a stack of bulletins was stationed at the inner door, but we dodged her and followed an arrow pointing to the nursery. We walked down a winding corridor lined with empty classrooms. Finally the strains of organ music were replaced by the shrieks of children playing on the other side of a windowless door. This would be the test, the moment when we'd actually have to interact with a parishioner and give our names and explain that Waylon had two mommies. I opened the door slowly.

"I know you!"

A green-haired woman was holding a baby next to the changing table. She was looking right past me, to Katy.

"My name is Cindy," she said. "And this is Mandy." She nodded toward a young, bespectacled dyke who was helping a toddler build a tower of brightly colored blocks.

"We're part of Kings-n-Things," Cindy continued, referencing the local drag king troupe.

"Oh, yeah," Katy said, smiling. "We played that show together!"

Of course. Of course she knows people here. We could fly to the moon and meet someone who knows her the minute we stepped off our spacecraft. I was bemused and relieved. Surely a church that put green-haired lesbians in charge of the childcare could not be all bad. Cindy and Mandy gave me confidence that I could leave Waylon without worrying that he'd be brainwashed by the time I returned.

Inside the sanctuary was warm and bright, with arcs of natural wood and beams of sunlight. We slid into the back pew just at the beginning of a sermon on environmental justice. It was peppered with useful facts and calls to civic-minded action—almost like a speech at a political rally, but with more references to the web of human connectedness. *I can handle this. I* am *handling this. I am sitting in a church pew right now and I am not horrified.* I was surprised and a little bit proud of my open-mindedness.

After the sermon, there was time for silent reflection. I closed my eyes and breathed deeply. *In. Out.* I felt like I'd been holding my breath for a long time, like my body and brain were starving for oxygen. *In. Out.* As the urgency of my need slowly subsided, I became aware of Katy's body next to mine. I could sense her suffering in the way she shifted her weight on the hard pew. In the silence, without Waylon or work or anything else vying for my attention, I felt patient and compassionate again. I wrapped my arm around her shoulder and squeezed with more warmth than I'd felt in weeks. *Yes, this.* I vowed to hold onto this peaceful, loving feeling, even if I had to keep coming back to church to find it.

I had come to the UUs to recruit voters, but perhaps the UUs would end up recruiting me.

CHAPTER 18

Hillbilly Heroin

ONE EVENING, AS I was driving home from work, something caught my eye. It was a bed frame in the window of a thrift shop. But not just any bed frame. It was a homemade bed frame in the shape of a train engine, with a smokebox and a cowcatcher and everything. It looked like something a super-handy grandparent had built for a little kid, like Waylon, who was obsessed with trains. That night, I mentioned the bed to Katy.

"We could ask Rachael to paint it red and gold, like Waylon's room." By noon the next day, she'd purchased it for $100 and paid someone at the store to haul it to our house. That was how our relationship was supposed to work. I was the idea guy and she was the get 'er done guy. That weekend, we bought a twin mattress and box spring to fit inside the train frame. Waylon finally had his big boy bed.

The transition to the big boy bed gave rise to a whole new bedtime ritual. Instead of reading picture books in the rocking chair, now we sat propped up on pillows in the bed. When the books were finished, Waylon usually wanted a made-up story, so I turned off the lamp and told him stories about bears and possums and pigs. By this time, his lids were getting heavy, but he resisted with all his might.

"I want Mommy."

"Mommy! Mommy!" we called in unison. "It's your turn."

As soon as we heard her stirring in the next room, Waylon wiggled into action.

"I'm going to hide. Tell Mommy that you lost me."

Waylon's idea of hiding was concealing himself in plain sight beneath the blanket.

"Mommy," I'd call, in an exaggerated sob. "I lost Waylon."

"What?" She shuffled into the room, ignoring the giggles that were issuing from the lumpy blanket. "You lost him? How *could* you?"

"I don't know," I woefully replied. "I just looked away for a second and then, poof, he was gone." More giggles.

"You lost my baby," Katy wailed. "Boo-hoo-hoo."

"Here I am, Mommy!" Waylon popped out from his hiding place with a big grin. I extricated myself from the bed, and Katy eased herself down into my place. "Did you know where I was? Did you think I was really gone?"

"I don't know," she said innocently. "I thought you might be."

"Let's hide from Mama!"

Waylon's insatiable appetite for hiding reminded me of Freud's story about the little boy who repeatedly threw his toy out of his crib, causing all the adults in the vicinity to search high and low for the missing object. Intrigued by the repetition, Freud surmised that throwing the toy away was a game that allowed the little boy to reenact the drama of separation from his mother. In the game, the pain of parting was closely followed by the pleasure of reunion. In the game, the child had control, and the pain of loss was trumped by the joy of mastery.

The pain in Katy's joints was growing worse. Some days her hands barely worked. Other days her neck seized up and she couldn't find any position that was bearable. The doctor did not think this was a reason to stop the treatment. He sent her to see a pain management doctor, who proposed a series of pain-blocking shots.

Early one morning, I dropped Katy at the clinic, then delivered Waylon to daycare. By the time I got back to the crowded waiting room, Katy had disappeared to the back. I took a seat and surveyed the scene from behind a tattered *Time* magazine. Across the aisle, a man with no teeth was sleeping in his chair, his lips flapping with each breath like a big-mouthed bass. To my right, a woman with swollen ankles was hunched forward, elbows on her knees. Every once in a while, she sighed like she was going into labor. To her right, a little boy and a little girl were entertaining themselves with a game of pushing and shoving. They had no toys or books, and the younger of the two, the little boy, was struggling to contain himself. He kept spilling onto the carpeted floor. "Mom, Mom, look!" he said. I was shocked to realize that he was addressing the hunched woman at my side. Her children were so young, she couldn't be that much older than I was, but pain or illness had rendered her prematurely ancient. I felt a wave of panic at the thought that this could be Katy's fate. I wanted very desperately to be in my office at the university, where no one moaned and time stayed in its proper place. I pulled my laptop out of my bag and tried to focus on my tasks for the day.

Finally, the nurse called me back to the recovery room. Katy was just coming out of the brief twilight state that they had induced in order to administer the shot.

"I was in a different room," she said groggily. "How did I get here?"

"We moved you after we gave you the shot, hon." The nurse was speaking slowly and patiently. Katy still looked confused. I flashed on the slack-mouthed man in the waiting room.

The only way to stay calm was to keep moving. I collected Katy's things and helped her to her feet. She leaned on my arm as we walked, slowly, to the car. I opened her door and settled her into the passenger seat, then buckled her seatbelt, just as I did for Waylon.

By the time we pulled onto Lamar Boulevard, Katy was beginning to look a little more lively. "The doctor gave me a prescription." She fished it out of her pocket. "Can you take me to get it filled?"

"What kind of prescription?"

"OxyContin."

"Hillbilly heroin?" Several years earlier, the *New York Times Magazine* had run a sensational feature on the time-release painkiller that could be crushed and snorted for a heroin-style high. As a joke, some friends had given Katy a prescription bottle full of candy with a handwritten label that said Hillbilly Heroin. At the time, the joke had seemed a little too close to home. Now it felt eerily prophetic.

"I thought the shot was supposed to help with the pain."

"It is. This is just for…just in case."

The panicky feeling again, like all my parts were spinning into outer space. The only way to keep them together was to focus on the next task, and then the next. I pulled the car into the Walgreen's parking lot, walked into the store, and handed the prescription through the window to the pharmacist.

Was I concerned about a former drug addict taking a highly addictive opiate? Yes. Did I try to stop it? No. Katy's pain had escalated from white noise to a constant jackhammering that made it nearly impossible to concentrate on anything else. I just wanted it to stop, and I was past the point of caring how it happened.

A few weeks later, I woke up at 6 a.m. Katy was already awake.

"Can you get my pills? My hands are hurting so bad, I can't open the bottle."

I got up and searched the large fleet of pill bottles on our dresser. Finally, I found the OxyContin and twisted the childproof lid. I measured out the pills and held them to her lips. She was so out of it that they dropped out of her mouth and spilled down her chest. I was feeling around in the bed for them, and I realized that Katy was lying on a towel. Even stranger, she wasn't wearing any underwear.

Katy's missing underwear scared me more than if she had been bleeding from her eyeballs. She *always* kept her boxer briefs on. She didn't even change in front of me, and she certainly didn't lie around with her lady parts hanging out.

"What happened last night?" I asked, shaking her shoulder.

"Wha?"

"What happened to your underwear?"

"Oh…uh," it was like she was remembering a dream. "I think I pissed myself." Her voice sounded very far away.

Like a jump cut in an experimental film, my mind skipped to the part of Simone de Beauvoir's memoir where the aging Jean Paul Sartre begins to lose control of his bladder. Each time de Beauvoir confronts him about his little accidents, he says, "some cats have peed on me," and she can't believe that her clear-eyed existentialist is reduced to such facile self-deception. In that moment, I knew just how Simone felt: *alone*.

I needed to focus on the task at hand. Clean sheets. They were in the cupboard in the bathroom. When I turned on the light to look for them, I noticed drops of blood on the bathroom tile. I followed the trail that ended at the toilet. More blood was smeared on the toilet seat.

I ran back to the bedroom. "Did you start your period last night?"

"Oh, yeah…" She sounded far away, like it didn't really matter either way. In the next room, I heard Waylon's feet hit the floor and start padding toward us. I made a dash for the bathroom, closing the door and then hastily wiping the floor and toilet seat with a washcloth. By the time I emerged, Waylon was in our room, clambering up onto our bed.

"Good morning!" I greeted him, trying to sound more cheerful than I felt. "I'm going to go get your milk. I'll be right back."

"Hide with me Mommy," he said in his sweet, high-pitched voice. He was trying to wiggle under the covers. I grabbed him out of the bed and swung him around to my hip. "Actually, let's go downstairs for milk."

Katy's eyes were closed and her mouth had fallen open.

CHAPTER 19

Plague of Moths

To HELP DEAL WITH the stress of Katy's illness, we started going to couples therapy. I came straight from the office, wearing smart Jackie O. sweaters and mod floral print skirts. Katy's workday started later than mine, so she walked in wearing what she called her "wallering" clothes: big, baggy concert tees and cut-off sweat pants. She lay on the therapist's couch like a beached whale—awkward and gray-faced and miserable.

The premise of the couple's therapy was that each of us had work to do. My job was to learn to express my needs directly. For too long, I'd been relying on Katy to read my mind. Instead of saying, "I want to go out with my friends," or "I need you to make dinner" or "I wish we could have sex," I tried to avoid potential conflict with a combination of subtle hints, psychic messaging, and sulking. If I never put my requests in words, then—theoretically—I never had to deal with rejection or disappointment. On the other hand, if I never put my requests into words, then—in actuality—I spent a lot of time feeling like a tearful martyr who gave and gave and gave.

Katy's job was to tolerate the fact that I still had needs, even when she was falling apart. Maybe this sounds obvious, but dissociation had always been Katy's first line of defense. It took a Herculean effort to cut through the fog of pain and anxiety. When she did manage to join me in the present moment, all she heard was criticism. *You're selfish. You're lazy. You're a bad parent and a terrible partner.* At that point, adrenaline pumping, she shifted gears, from dissociative to defensive.

Our sessions lurched from recrimination to accusation.

"I need a break from taking care of other people."

114

"Do you think I'm enjoying this? I'm just trying to get through the day."

"I just want you to sympathize with what I'm going through."

"What you're going through? What *you're* going through?"

Our therapist, Claire, handed us a Mexican-tile coaster and instructed us to pass the "talking tile" between us. When one partner held the coaster, the other partner had to listen without interrupting. When the coaster changed hands, it was the other person's turn to take the floor. The whole exercise was a depressing reminder of how far we'd fallen since the night when we'd laid next to each other on the rock at Mt. Bonnell, excitedly finishing each other's sentences.

Therapy was supposed to be like an emotional lance—you drained the pus of festering feelings, and then you could heal. So why did I feel like shit after each session? Why did Katy look more grim and gray? In between appointments, we danced around our feelings, carefully avoiding any interaction that would rip the scab before we were back in the safety of Claire's office. Actually, it didn't feel safe, even there, but at least there was a container, a place to store the bitterness and betrayal until the next week.

In the midst of this emotional standoff, our house was visited by a plague of pantry moths. Every time I opened a cabinet, I was greeted by the fluttering of small brown wings. Some clung to the inside of the pantry door, and an ever-increasing colony hung from the tops of the shelves like tiny bats in a kitchen-sized cave. When I went to make pancakes or cornbread, I found them burrowed deep inside canisters of dry goods. They had an uncanny ability to breach hermetically sealed plastic bags.

I guessed I could dispatch the unwanted visitors with bug spray, but I didn't like the idea of toxic chemicals clinging to my foodstuffs any more than I liked pantry moths. Besides, our house was situated above an aquifer, and I had a thing about not poisoning the groundwater. So

I visited the eco-friendly hardware store for advice on nontoxic moth management. They sent me home with a flimsy piece of sticky cardboard soaked in pantry-moth pheromones. When I opened the pantry and peered around for a place to put it, brazen moths flapped their wings in my face. I slammed the door shut and leaned against it, rubbing the ticklish traces of moth wings from my eyes and nose.

I wanted to shake my fist at the heavens and cry, "What next?!?" But before the words left my lips, the phone rang.

It was my mother. She was coming for a visit.

I knew she'd be incredibly helpful, and yet I was filled with dread. I didn't want anyone to see how tense things were between Katy and me. I was embarrassed by our dirty, moth-ridden kitchen and the generalized domestic chaos that had descended since Katy got sick. When I imagined my mother pulling in the driveway, I saw our house through her eyes. The un-mowed weeds in the front yard, the discarded toys on the porch—all the things I'd been ignoring in order to focus on the crisis at hand—suddenly started to scream for my attention.

When I was growing up, my mother made pickles and preserves and applesauce. She baked cookies and decorated cakes. She sent me and my sister to elementary school in handmade gingham prairie skirts and tucked us into bed wearing home-sewn nightgowns that matched her own.

She had too much energy for a mere family of four. During the rare periods when she wasn't working outside the home, she'd lie in wait for me after school, eager to list her accomplishments: "I cleaned the cobwebs off the ceiling, and then I baked muffins with leftover cereal and reorganized the linen closet..." Overwhelmed by the sheer force of her domestic industry, I would flee to my room, hoping that homework could save me from home improvement.

My mother's homemaking skills may have been forged in the kitchens of her Mormon girlhood, but her perfectionism was honed in the aftermath of her parents' apostasy. When my grandparents left the church of the Latter Day Saints, every aspect of their lives became a potential reflection of their religious choices. If they failed—in business or in love, in cleanliness or good citizenship—their hard times might be interpreted as God's wrath. My grandmother was determined not to give any grist to the Mormon gossip mill. She kept her kitchen sparkling clean and set the table with starched linens. She eschewed hard liquor and even scrambled to hide the coffeepot when one of her seven sisters pulled into the driveway. She refused to let my mother wear makeup and dressed her only daughter in modest, muted colors. Her life was a carefully curated monument to respectability.

As Mom grew older, she chafed under this regime of propriety. She bought a racy leopard-print belt to accent her bland beige clothes. She escaped to college, married a Catholic, and attended consciousness-raising sessions. But she could never quite silence Grandma's insistent voice in her head: *Judge first, judge often, lest ye be judged.*

The night before Mom was due to arrive, I swept and mopped the wood floors. Waylon was a messy eater, and we usually let our dachshund, Little Eddy, serve as the vacuum cleaner for all the stray food that found its way to the floor. Eddy was pretty efficient at finding wayward Cheerios. He'd even been known to lick up large spills. But he didn't do anything about the sand. Every day, Waylon came home from preschool with sand in his shoes, his socks, his hair—even the creases of his skin. We had taken to undressing him on the back porch before he came inside, but he continued to shed grains of sand from the backdoor to the bathtub, and his dirty clothes were a big ball of grit.

I ran the mop over Waylon's sand trail one last time and then dialed my mom.

"I'll pick you up at the airport," I told her. "But we'll have to swing back by the office because I have a meeting at 3."

"Is there a refrigerator at your office? I'm bringing a frozen chicken in my suitcase."

"Mom, we have chickens in Texas."

"They were on sale at Bashas'. I'll just take a cab to your house."

When I arrived home from work that evening, I was greeted by the soothing aroma of roasted chicken and the disturbing sight of my sixty-year-old mother on her hands and knees, scrubbing the kitchen floor.

"Mom, I just mopped yesterday!"

"There's just so much sand," she said, pushing a strand of perfectly coiffed blonde hair back into place. I felt a twinge of defensiveness, but I pushed it aside. I didn't want to devolve into a bratty teenager the moment my mother arrived.

Later, after a delicious home-cooked dinner, Mom gave Waylon a bath and read him a bedtime story. I was grateful to have a few minutes to check on Katy. She had barely eaten at dinner and had spoken so little that I was afraid Mom would think she was rude.

"Ugh," Katy moaned. She was lying sprawled on her stomach in our bed. "My belly hurts so bad. It's like I'm being stabbed with a knife."

The pain killers were making Katy constipated. Not just a little garden-variety constipation, but more like I-can't-believe-I'm-not-toxic constipation. I knew it was really bad, because I'd opened Katy's laptop one day to find that she'd been searching *diverticulitis* and other colon-related disasters.

I stepped into the bathroom and mixed up a glass of what we called "poop potion," an extra-strength laxative that the pain-management doctor had recommended. I'd been doing the same thing every night for a week, and I was beginning to feel really panicky. How would I know when things had crossed a line? Was she in imminent danger? Should we be heading to the hospital right now?

In a practical sense, my mother's arrival made it easier to contemplate a trip to the emergency room. At least we had someone to stay with Waylon if we needed to leave in a hurry. From an emotional standpoint, my mother's presence made it even more difficult to figure out what to do. If we went to the emergency room, I'd have to tell her the whole sordid story—the joint pain, the opiates, the constipation. I wasn't eager to have my mother all up in our shit (or the lack thereof).

I sat on the side of the bed and stroked Katy's back. Her moaning subsided a bit, and she seemed like she might fall asleep. I decided to wait and see if things got worse.

I emerged from the bedroom with my old smile pasted in place.

"Can I make you a cup of tea?" I asked. I was determined to be a good host, even though my mind was back upstairs at Katy's bedside.

"That would be nice," Mom said, taking off her shoes and curling up in an armchair in the living room. In addition to spoiling her grandson, I knew that this was what she had come to Texas for—a little quality mother-daughter time. I was exhausted; I really just wanted to climb in bed, but I owed her this much, especially since she'd scrubbed my floors.

I handed her a cup of lemon tea and settled into the couch. Mom proceeded to fill me in on the latest exploits of her friends and neighbors back home in Fountain Hills, Arizona. Many of these updates were united by a single theme: people made poor choices.

"I told her that you have to mix the dry ingredients separately, but she didn't listen," Mom concluded one such anecdote. "Her cookies came out like salty little hockey pucks."

I stifled a yawn. In the flood of minutiae, I had lost track of the identity of this particular baking bimbo. Were we talking about her coworker? Or was it her cousin?

"Oh *well*," Mom concluded, giving the stoic little shrug that said she was powerless in the face of other peoples' stupidity.

I thought we might be about to wrap up, but just as I started to say goodnight, she shifted her tone to indicate that it was time for a real heart-to-heart. "So!" she said brightly, "how are *you*?"

It was a scene we'd played out so often that I'd come to think of our roles in terms of an old *Peanuts* comic strip. Mom was silver-tongued Lucy, enticing me to kick the football, and I was dimwitted, gullible

Charlie Brown. "C'mon, Chuck," she said, "just kick the ball. I promise I won't move it this time!"

I always fell for it. Mom would encourage me to share what was "really going on" in my life, and I would spill my guts about hopes and fears, triumphs and disappointments. As soon as I got really present and vulnerable, then all of a sudden—*Wump!*

She'd change the subject.

It wasn't her fault. She'd grown up in a family that was terminally uncomfortable with messy feelings. I knew she was hungry for deeper connection. I could see it in her eyes and feel it in her insistent attempts at mother-daughter bonding. But as soon as anything unscripted started to unfold, she fled to more familiar territory: her habitual list of personal accomplishments, household hints, and complaints.

Now her unanswered question hung in the air. It was so tempting to unburden myself, to say that Katy was really bad and I didn't even know how bad and I wasn't sure how much longer we could keep it together with the kid and work and new symptoms showing up every day. I wanted to put my head on her shoulder and surrender to the sobs that were rising in my chest.

"I'm not going to lie," I said, swallowing hard. "It's been difficult..."

She tilted her head and made a listening face.

"...but I think we're managing."

"That's good, sweetie. I worry about you. You know, I could get some spray that would take care of those moths."

"No, thanks. I'm trying not to use pesticides. I got a glue trap. It's just going to take a while," I said, trying to sound confident. "Thanks for the yummy dinner, Mom."

I headed upstairs with a mixture of relief and regret. I was glad I hadn't spilled my guts only to feel the disappointment of having the whole mess swept under the rug. But I couldn't help wishing that things were different.

Two nights later, I was awakened by a clattering sound downstairs. I looked at the clock on my bedside table. It was 5 a.m. I started to fall back asleep, but then I heard the noise again. There was definitely something going on in the kitchen. I pulled myself out of bed and tiptoed to the top of the stairs. A horrifying smell, a mix of chemicals and perfume, drifted up to meet me.

"Mom!" I said, charging down the steps. "What are you doing?"

She was standing in front of the open pantry in her pink satin nightie, a graveyard of dead moths gathered at her feet.

"It's organic!" she said preemptively. She was holding something behind her back like five-year-old caught with a forbidden cookie.

I held out my hand and she reluctantly handed over the bottle of Raid "Earth Expressions" bug spray.

"No," I said sternly, "Uh-uh."

Mom looked extremely sheepish. I averted my eyes like a sullen teenager. *Gah, Mom, why can't you understand me? Do you even listen when I'm talking to you? You always think you know best. Now I'll have to keep Waylon out of the kitchen and wipe down all the cans and…* As I was enumerating all the extra work she'd created, a traitorous feeling poked through the asphalt of my ire: *At least the Goddamn moths are gone.*

Relief blossomed into amusement. Even in my anger, I had to admit it was kind of hilarious to think of Mom spraying under cover of darkness, like a sneaky nightgown-wearing ninja. I felt a smile tugging at the corners of my mouth.

"I was just trying to help," she said quietly.

"I know, Mom." I put down the Raid and gave her a hug. "I know."

Over the next three days, Mom washed and folded all our laundry. She ironed my work clothes, baked cookies with Waylon, and filled our freezer with homemade meatballs. By the time I took her to the airport, we were both exhausted—Mom from the whirlwind of housework and me from stress of imagining every dust bunny and pill bottle through her eyes. I shuddered to think what tales she'd tell the folks back home. *The sand! The moths! The household sloth!* But maybe she'd just tell them how cute her grandson was.

"Bye, Mom. Thanks so much for all of your help." Despite my weariness, I was truly grateful. Her exertions had carved out a precious bit of breathing room—a few more minutes to sleep in the morning or relax with Katy and Waylon before dinner—that I would relish for weeks to come.

"Oh, sweetie, I just wish I lived closer. You've got a lot on your plate right now."

I hugged her goodbye with tears in my eyes. Even though we couldn't really talk about it, I knew that Mom knew I was struggling. And I knew she'd be back—with a chicken in her suitcase and a scrub brush in her purse—whenever I needed a helping hand.

CHAPTER 20

Crawford

ONE EVENING I WALKED into our room to find Katy uncharacteristically upright in bed. The television was turned off, and she was peering intently at her laptop.

"Whatcha doin'?" I asked cautiously. Despite my strenuous objections, Katy sometimes visited online forums where interferon users posted dire accounts of terrible side effects.

"I'm reading about Cindy Sheehan."

"Cool!" I scooted onto the bed so that I could read over her shoulder, excited about the opportunity to talk about something besides symptoms.

Cindy Sheehan was the mother of Casey Sheehan, a 24-year-old soldier who had been killed in Iraq. In the months after her son's death, the bereaved mother met with President Bush, but she wasn't comforted by the President's evasive answers about the purpose of the war. Using her maternal grief as a megaphone, she began to make public demands for Bush to explain U.S. military involvement in Iraq. The White House ignored her requests, but Sheehan refused to let the question fade from the public spotlight. When Bush embarked for a 6-week vacation at his ranch in Crawford, Texas, Sheehan and her supporters began occupying a small strip of public land nearby. Now one of Bush's neighbors had donated some land to the cause, and antiwar activists had begun to pilgrimage to "Camp Casey."

"They're calling for a day of action against the war." Katy turned to face me. "I think we should go."

"Do you really think you're up to it?"

"Yeah," she said, "I think I can handle it."

Despite my apprehensions about the heat and the stress, I didn't need to be asked twice. By this time, the Bush administration was refusing to let reporters take pictures of soldiers' coffins coming home from the battlefield, and the mainstream media seemed content to let the war fade from Americans' consciousness. Once a week, I forced myself to look up the Iraqi civilian death toll on a website that compiled numbers from various human rights organizations, because I needed a number to give meaning to the dry, repetitive NPR stories that chronicled bombs exploding in villages and markets and roadways.

Watching death tolls mount while sending emails to my Republican senators was making me feel powerless and depressed. But Cindy Sheehan refused to let her loss be forgotten. She was determined to wrest some meaning from her son's death, and, in a sentimental culture obsessed with stories of personal adversity and triumph, she seemed like one of the few anti-war voices who could actually be heard. I wanted to support her. With my limited window of time and opportunity, I wanted to join forces with other people and do something that actually might make a difference.

On Saturday morning, we loaded up the car with water, sunscreen, diapers, and snacks. We stopped to pick up our friend Rachael, the lead singer and mastermind behind Katy's old band. I was relieved to have Rachael along, because Katy tended to rally when friends were around. Besides, if Katy broke down, I'd have one more adult around to help me figure out what to do. (My mind couldn't help running scenarios—how far was Crawford from the nearest hospital? Could they airlift her out of there if they needed to? How would a rural doctor deal with Katy's gender?)

But this morning, Katy looked almost healthy. She was wearing a khaki sun hat, as if this journey into deep Republican territory required special protective gear. From the backseat, I couldn't follow her conversation with Rachael, because the stretch of interstate between Austin and Waco was under construction. We were hurtling 80 miles an hour over raw, ridged concrete. I spaced out on the insistent beat of tires bouncing over a rough road.

The time signature of parenthood is supposed to be progress. Baby sits up, learns to walk, learns to talk. The crib is replaced by the big boy bed. One year's school portrait is supplanted by the next. You measure the months and years in inch marks on the wall.

Since Katy got sick, time had lurched forward and back until I lost all sense of it. A mere four months had passed, yet I could barely remember a time when things had been different. I hardly dared to hope for a future that was different from the brutal, unbearable now. Today was a welcome respite, but I couldn't shake the feeling of impending doom.

Just before we turned off the interstate toward Crawford, Katy pulled into a convenience store to pee and grab some drinks. I needed to take advantage of this moment alone with Rachael. I wanted to say, "your friend isn't doing well," or something along those lines, but I could never tell how much our friends knew. I couldn't tell if it was obvious that we were struggling. I had grown up in a family where hard times were considered private and shameful, and some primitive part of me still believed that bad things only happened to bad people. *What if Rachael thinks I'm being melodramatic? What if Katy's sudden burst of energy cancels out my concerns? Will it seem selfish to ask for help when the observable evidence suggests that Katy is holding her own?* These same questions arose every time we were with friends, chewing away at the sense of community and common purpose that I'd felt since our wedding.

I dipped a whole-wheat cracker in some peanut butter and handed it to Waylon in his car seat.

"Waylon really loves peanut butter," I babbled.

As we approached Crawford, red-white-and-blue billboards welcomed us to the home of George W. Bush. The center of town was packed. Traffic on the two-lane main street slowed to a crawl. Counter-demonstrators were flocking to Crawford too, and every other car seemed to be an SUV with a smug "W" bumper sticker. The apex of their activity was the old-timey store front of the Yellow Rose, a convenience store-turned-Bush-souvenir shop with American flags and signs proclaiming support for the troops.

We followed the beater cars with anti-war bumper stickers. A few miles beyond the town, a mammoth, multi-peaked white tent rose up out of the cotton fields. We parked on the side of the road and walked with a steady stream of people past a long row of cars. To our left was a field of white crosses commemorating all the American soldiers who had died in Iraq and Afghanistan. I prayed that Waylon wouldn't notice them, because I couldn't imagine how I would explain that vast swath of death. The frog in the road had been hard enough, but what about thousands of sons and daughters?

At the edge of the tent, a grandmotherly woman reminded us to drink lots of water in the 100 heat. As I scanned around to get my bearings, I saw Joan Baez emerge from a porta-potty and help herself to the economy-size hand sanitizer that someone had thoughtfully positioned just outside the door. I was in awe.

Inside the tent were rows and rows of folding chairs facing a low stage. Occasionally someone famous would take the stage to talk or sing, but the majority of speakers were just plain folks, parents and siblings of the dead. We found seats near the side of the stage. I spread a blanket on the ground for Waylon and unpacked his toys from the diaper bag. Baez sang "take what you need and leave the rest, but you should never have taken the very best." Parents spoke of the shining promise shown by their dead sons and daughters. These moms and dads were not life-long radicals. They were people who had been radicalized by loss, and they inveighed against greed and empire in the astonished tones of adults whose world view has been torn and shifted. Tears trickled steadily down my cheek. I felt a connection with these men and women whose families had been interrupted. The comforting fictions of progress and security had been yanked away, but they had come here, under this tent, to try to remake the world.

Baez sang "The Ballad of Joe Hill." The eerie chorus filled the tent: "I never died said he. I never died said he."

I desperately wanted the words of the song to be true. I hoped that all the suffering and effort would make some kind of difference, that these people would have the comfort of knowing that they wrested something meaningful from their children's deaths.

More tears. I left Waylon with Katy and walked out under the midday sun. Between the tent and the field of white crosses, there was a makeshift wall with names and photos of all the soldiers who had died in Iraq. My friend Doug's brother had been killed early in the war. I ran my finger down the list until I located David Bernstein. I pictured his brother and his parents. At church I'd learned about the Tibetan Buddhist practice of *tonglen* meditation, and now I tried to breathe in the suffering of this family and all the families who had lost loved ones on both sides of the war. On the exhale, I imagined wrapping all the mourners in a blanket of comfort and love.

When I turned around, I saw Katy and Waylon were kicking a beach ball in the brown grass behind me. Waylon wasn't quite coordinated enough to stop the ball in motion, so Katy sent it toward him with a gentle tap. Waylon watched with grave concentration as it rolled toward him and squealed with excitement each time he managed to kick it back in her direction.

I wonder if he'll remember this day when he's older, after she's gone? The thought floated up to the surface of my consciousness and hung there. Despite the heat of the day, I shivered in the shadow that it cast.

It was the first time I admitted that Katy might be dying.

At the end of the day, after a heaping plate of barbecue and potato salad from the buffet line at the back of the tent, we headed back to the station wagon and navigated back through Crawford, past crowds of Bush supporters who had bussed in from all over the country. The thought of meeting pumped-up war hawks on a country road made me nervous, and I was relieved when we hit I-35 and I heard the steady sound of our tires on the highway. I was in the backseat with Waylon, trying to coax him into sleep, when I realized that the thud of the tires was growing louder and more percussive.

I leaned toward the front.

"Do we have a flat tire?" I asked over the din.

Katy looked at Rachael, and the two of them listened carefully.

"Well, hell," Katy said.

We pulled off onto the shoulder and Katy and Rach got out and walked around to the back. A minute later, I heard the trunk open, and turned to see Katy rummaging under the mat for the jack and spare.

"Where's Mommy?" Waylon asked sleepily.

"She just has to fix the tire," I said. Outside, speeding cars passed inches from Waylon's door, causing the car to shudder and shake. I wrapped my arm around his car seat and kissed his head.

"It's okay. Everything's going to be fine." But Waylon had already fallen back asleep. I was talking to myself.

CHAPTER 21

Katrina

ON MONDAY, HURRICANE KATRINA made landfall and the levees broke. On Tuesday George Bush spent the final night of his vacation in Crawford. On Wednesday, Camp Casey was disbanded. A group of anti-war veterans loaded up all the supplies—bottles of water, packets of Emergen-C—and drove them to Louisiana shelters. Bush flew over New Orleans on Air Force One.

Katy took to her bed, watching CNN every moment that she wasn't with Waylon or at work. When I came home from the office, we spoke in hushed tones until Waylon was in bed. Once he was asleep, we yelled at the television, railing against the indifference that was leaving so many poor, black people stranded.

"Oh my God," Katy moaned in agony. "What's taking so long?"

I was haunted by the parents with young children. I couldn't stop thinking of all the things I took for granted, like clean diapers and fresh milk. The thought of not being able to get them made my heart beat fast, like a nervous rabbit. When reporters spoke of "looting," I imagined how desperate I would be to provide for my family. I hated the media for pathologizing black people, and I hated the authorities who prioritized law and order over rescue missions.

"Something's wrong with my mouth," Katy said when we finally turned off the TV. "Look. It's all broken out in canker sores."

We had just watched a story about a family who pulled themselves into the attic and then clawed their way through the roof while the water was rising around them. Canker sores seemed meaningless in comparison.

"Hmm," I said, feigning sympathy.

Survivors from New Orleans were pouring into Austin. The city opened up the convention center as a temporary shelter. They needed volunteers to help connect the displaced with food and clothes and FEMA benefits. Many of my friends were volunteering. I wanted to volunteer too, but I couldn't bring myself to take time off. Work felt like the only stable thing left in my life, and I was afraid I might lose my shit if I deviated from my eight to five routine. At five o' clock, I rushed to the daycare center to pick up Waylon before they closed, and then I rushed home to make dinner.

Katy pushed away her plate after a few bites. She looked ready to get up from the table and escape to the bedroom.

"You have to eat," I scolded. "You have to take a break from watching the news."

"It's not that," she said. "It's just my mouth. It really hurts. My tongue feels rough, like it's covered in little bumps."

I listened with only part of my mind. New symptoms arose almost daily, and I had to maintain a certain distance in order to stay calm. After dinner, I gave Waylon his bath, read him two stories, and tucked him in bed.

"Mommy, it's your turn!"

Katy heaved herself out of bed and shuffled down the hall to Waylon's room. While she sang him to sleep, I busied myself with filling a box full of supplies to donate to the evacuees: pillows, blankets, towels. I scanned the bathroom cabinet for unopened soaps and shampoos. My eyes fell on a bottle of mouthwash. The symptoms that I'd half heard at dinner echoed in my mind. "My tongue feels all rough and bumpy."

A name dislodged itself from a dusty shelf in my brain. It was a diagnosis gleaned from AIDS memoirs and documentaries.

Katy tiptoed out of Waylon's room and closed the door quietly behind her. I was waiting.

"It's thrush," I said. "You have thrush."

Thrush might not be life threatening, but it was associated in my mind with the end of life. From that moment on, I couldn't help thinking ahead to Katy's death. *How much does a funeral cost? Can I borrow money to pay for it? How long will it take me to sell the house? Can I move in with my sister?* It was dry and actuarial, but the laundry list of questions kept me from focusing on the ache in my heart.

Katy still dragged her tired body to the office Monday through Thursday. In retrospect, it seems strange that we didn't apply for disability or find some other way for her to take a break. We needed her income, sure, but that wasn't the whole story. As long as she kept going to the office, our days had some semblance of normalcy. As long as Katy kept working, she was still providing for her family, still helping people who needed her. She was still a part of the world.

Most nights, when she came home from the office, she could barely stay upright at the dinner table. I didn't imagine that her ashen face and fluttering eyelids were inspiring confidence in her clients, and I wasn't surprised when she told me that some of them had begun to worry that she might be terminally ill. Of course, as therapy clients, they were supposed to project their most primal fears on the screen of her face, but still, it was oddly comforting to think that there were other people, like me, who depended upon her and were beginning to wonder how much longer she'd be around.

I was surprised to discover that I could consider these grim questions while going through the motions of daily life. It was like my mind had two parallel tracks. I might be thumping melons at the grocery store or writing on the chalkboard in my classroom, but inside I was thinking *what songs should I play at her funeral?*

A new semester had begun. I was teaching a writing course called Rhetoric of Environmental Issues. Long before Katrina, I had decided to focus the class on the so-called "chemical corridor," the chain of chemical refineries between Houston and New Orleans. The syllabus was designed to help my mostly white, privileged students understand that geographical legacy of slavery and its connection to the mostly poor, black people who lived and worked in the toxic environs of the chemical plants. When I was planning the course, I'd feared that the white students might become defensive when confronted with evidence of inequality. After the storm, after days of indifference and inaction in the face of black suffering, my fears changed. What hope could I offer my students? What possibility of a way forward? Martin Luther King Jr. had said that the "arc of the moral universe is long, but it bends toward justice." Now the arc seemed broken, bent into a circle and doomed to repeat itself.

Because much of New Orleans was still underwater, the University of Texas agreed to admit students from University of New Orleans, Loyola and Tulane on a temporary basis. One of the displaced students, a young white woman, was placed in my class. She showed up the first week, sat by herself, and barely participated in the icebreaker exercises I'd designed to help students connect. I struggled to manifest warmth and welcome, but the course material was unintentionally chilling. We watched a depression-era documentary about the Mississippi River. Seventy-year-old images of swollen logs on rushing water recalled the fresh horror of dead bodies floating down flooded streets. I drew a map of the Gulf coast on the board. I looked back at the class. The woman from New Orleans was staring into space.

She kept to herself for the rest of the semester, choosing paper topics that had nothing to do with Louisiana and revealing nothing of her experience in class discussion. I worried that I was failing her, but I also respected her desire to remain apart. Connection with other people requires presence, and sometimes you have to leave the present moment in order to survive it.

CHAPTER 22

Pink Salt, White Tree

ONCE A WEEK, KATY went to see a massage therapist who studied with a Maya master healer in Belize. In 30 years of bodywork, the therapist said she'd never seen anything like what was happening to Katy's body: the soft tissues were hardening up to the point of impenetrability. It was almost like she was growing a turtle shell.

It felt like an apt metaphor for our physical connection. The more panicked I felt, the more I withdrew. In order to stay calm and keep moving, I had to stop letting every setback and symptom touch my heart. And the more pain Katy felt, the less she wanted to be touched. Even though she woke me with her moaning in the middle of the night, she winced and pulled away if I tried to rub her back or stroke her arm. Lately she had developed neuropathy, which manifested as pain and numbness in her feet. Sometimes even the touch of the bed sheet under her heels was unbearable.

When Katy told me that a friend had recommended reflexology, I was skeptical, but I kept my comments about a lack of clinical evidence to myself. Things were already tense between us, and Donna Koonce was footing the bill for all of Katy's nontraditional treatments, so I just made noncommittal "hmm" noises when she described her first meeting with Lars, the scion of an old Austin family who practiced reflexology in his down-at-the-heels mansion on a hill.

I hoped that ignoring Lars would make him go away, but soon Katy's conversation was peppered with Lars-isms. Lars told me to drink wheat grass. Lars told me to buy turmeric capsules. Lars thinks I should only eat raw foods. Lars, Lars, Lars—I hated the sound of his name. In truth,

I think I was jealous that Katy was so infatuated with him and that he alone seemed to be able to touch her in a way that afforded some relief.

A few weeks later, Katy came home with a book about Himalayan crystal salt.

"Lars told me to read it," she said, "he thinks it could really help."

After her weekly Thursday night shot, she retired to bed with the book in hand. Throughout the weekend, she alternated between dozing on the couch and reading about the healing properties of pink salt.

"Babe, check this out!" I put down the pile of laundry I had gathered from the floor of our room and scanned a poorly punctuated passage about Himalayan crystal salt's ability to destroy negative energy and create positive vibrations. It was about as coherent as the label on a bottle of Dr. Bronner's liquid soap.

"Interesting," I said, rushing from the room to avoid further discussion.

On the Sunday after Katrina made landfall, the sermon at the Unitarian Universalist church was about connections between the war in Iraq and the failure of the levees in New Orleans. Rev. Loehr inveighed against military spending, which had sapped critical dollars for infrastructure. As a result, he said bitterly, people were dying at home and abroad.

It was a relief to hear someone give vent to his righteous anger. Attending UU church was kind of like listening to Air America, the lefty talk radio station—only with choir music and free childcare.

During the meditation time, I thought about the faces of the people I'd seen on TV—a small boy who was separated from his parents, a woman searching for news of her neighbor. I practiced mentally enveloping each one of them in a cloud of love and compassion.

Next, I thought about Katy. On Friday, her doctor's office had called with bad news: according to her latest blood work, the virus was not responding as they'd hoped. In fact, her viral load had actually surged since she started the treatment. The doctor wanted to meet with her, and she was dreading the prospect of switching to a new combination therapy with its own fresh hell of side effects.

I pictured Katy's face and practiced surrounding her with my cloud of compassion and love. It was a scientific fact that you could increase your capacity for compassion through practice. I'd read about a study where they put electrodes on the skulls of Buddhist monks and watched them meditate.

In the final seconds of meditation time, I repeated a silent plea: *please let me be more patient, please let me feel more compassion. Please, please.* It was the closest I'd come to prayer.

I thought I was hiding my panic fairly well, but apparently I wasn't all that poker-faced. Or maybe my attempts to stay calm made me seem hard-hearted, because Katy started hiding symptoms from me. It was only when I pressed her about the Himalayan crystal salt that she admitted that the constipation had returned. She hadn't pooped in almost two weeks, and Lars had prescribed the salt as a laxative.

"Babe, can you make me a glass of sole?"

Sole, I had learned, was the name for a solution of water and Himalayan crystal salt—and the occasion for plenty of bad puns.

"How much do I put?"

"A tablespoon in about this much water." She held her fingers three inches apart.

I shuffled reluctantly to the kitchen. When I returned, Katy had closed her eyes.

"Why isn't it bad for you, like regular salt?" I asked, waving the cup of warm water in the vicinity of her face.

"It has a different molecular structure than table salt," she answered, as if reading the book had turned her into a chemistry major overnight.

For the next few days, Katy was nauseous all the time. Her fingers swelled up like sausages, she couldn't wear her wedding ring, and her features looked lost in her big, bloated face.

"It's moon face," she moaned, referring to the most-feared side effect of the steroids the doctor had prescribed for the inflammation in her joints.

I was pretty sure that the culprit was not steroids, but rather Himalayan crystal salt. In desperation, I grabbed the book away from her and began to read the hateful thing in earnest. It took me a while to find the practical information I sought.

"How much crystal salt have you been taking?"

"One tablespoon...twice a day."

"It says here that the recommended dose is 1 teaspoon—that's like a third of a tablespoon."

"Oh." She looked surprised and confused.

I confiscated the book and the bottle of pink crystals.

"No more salt, Sweetie. No more." It sounded like I was speaking to my toddler instead of my spouse, but the vehemence in my voice was a measure of how shaky I felt inside. Despite our differences, I had always looked up to Katy. She was older and wiser and more like the person I wanted to be. She was the Captain, and I the First Mate. Now I was beginning to doubt her ability to steer the ship. It looked like I needed to step up to the wheel.

I forced Katy to go see the doctor. He gave her another prescription and warned that if the new medicine didn't get things moving, she might have to go to the hospital for an enema. I knew right away that a hospital enema was a non-starter, and I wondered that the doctor couldn't see what was right in front of his face. As a trans person, Katy had experienced too much shame about her body to allow it to be exposed in that way. Katy would allow her intestine to explode rather than submit to such indignity. *If I have to have emergency surgery,* I could imagine her thinking, *at least I'll be unconscious.*

Back home, Katy swallowed the medicine and disappeared into the bathroom. She was determined not to emerge until something happened. I sat on the couch with Waylon and watched a *Thomas the Train* video, privately imagining how a trip to the emergency room might unfold. Would they recognize me as her wife? What if something terrible happened? Would I be allowed to make decisions? Would people be nice to her? Or would they treat her like a gender-ambiguous, drug-addicted freak? I played out all the possible scenarios over and over in my mind. Finally, Katy emerged from the bathroom, looking tired. "Well," she said, "It's better than nothing." I breathed a sigh of relief. No hospital today.

It was the first weekend in November, and I had hoped that we'd be able to do something seasonal together—maybe drive out to the Texas Hill Country, like we used to do. As Friday turned to Saturday, it seemed clear that an outing was not in the cards. The constipation crisis had abated, but it was an effort to even get Katy to come downstairs to the living room and watch Waylon while he played with his toy trains.

We had recently traded our coffee table for a 4 x 6 train table with room to build loops and figure eights out of interlocking wooden track. In theory, it was a way for Waylon to amuse himself, but, in actuality, he always wanted one of us to get down on the floor and help.

"Mommy, will you play trains with me?" he asked. Katy's eyes were closed, and she muttered something incomprehensible.

"I'll play," I said, plopping down next to him. "What's happening?"

Playing with Waylon consisted largely of listening to an endless set of ground rules about how the game could be played. "Thomas and James are having a race," he explained.

"What about Percy?" Percy was my favorite, a neurotic little green engine. I picked him up and waved him in Waylon's direction.

"No, Percy's not in the game."

"I feel put upon," I said, wheeling Percy into the station house and quoting an episode of *Thomas the Tank Engine* that we'd all watched a million times.

"No, Mama," Waylon said firmly. "That's not how it goes."

My job was to use my nimble adult fingers to piece the track together. Since Waylon was in full control of the narrative, my mind had plenty of room to wander while we played. *I should stop acting like a put-upon-Percy,* I thought. *I should stop waiting for Katy to get well in order to do family stuff. I'm not confined to the house. I'm not helpless. I can cheer this place up and make new memories for Waylon.*

"Waylon, let's get your shoes, we're going to Target."

"Can I get a new train?"

"Yes, for sure!" If a $10 train was all it took to recruit an enthusiastic companion, then it seemed like a small price to pay.

Inside the store was bright and cheery. *I feel better already,* I thought, lifting Waylon into the cart. Our first stop was the toy section, where we studied the selection of toy trains.

"How about Duncan? You don't have Duncan."

"Nooooooo."

"Here's Mavis, she looks like a nice engine."

"Let me see." I grabbed Mavis off the rack. Waylon studied her small plastic features with great seriousness, then handed her back. "Uh-uh."

It seemed like an eternity, but it was probably only fifteen minutes later when the deliberations finally concluded and I could push the cart to our real destination: the Christmas aisle. It was only the beginning of the month, and the Christmas mania was still confined to a tasteful corner of the store. At first my hopes faltered. Then, tucked away at the end of a row, I saw what I had come for.

"See that tree up there, Waylon?"

He reluctantly tore his eyes away from the train in his hands.

"What's different about it?" I asked.

He looked up and down the aisle of artificial trees. "It's white?"

"That's right! And a white tree is the kind Mommy always had at her house when she was growing up. We're going to surprise her with it!"

We drove up and down the aisles until we found a Target employee who could help us. I gave him the number on the box, and he instructed me to proceed to checkout. Waylon and I rolled through the store chanting, "White trees are better than green trees, white trees are better than green trees." When it was our turn at the register, I told the cashier that we were expecting a tree. She made a call, and presently a teenager appeared with a large box on a flatbed cart.

Gulp. It was a very large box.

Too late to back out now, I'd already paid. The young man followed me to the parking lot, where I'm sure he was very surprised to find that I was driving a Prius instead of some vehicle with the capacity to haul a very large box. I strapped Waylon into the car seat and moved some things out of my trunk, as if clearing the junk away would somehow increase the size of the trunk door. "Do you think it might fit if we turned it sideways?"

The young man looked dubious, but he tried a variety of angles, none of which made the box any smaller.

"You know what? You can just leave it here next to the car. I'll figure it out."

"Are you sure ma'am?"

"Yes, yes, I'll call my friend."

When Katy answered the phone, she sounded like she'd just woken up from a deep sleep. "Huh?"

"Hi. I'm at Target with Waylon, and I just bought a Christmas tree—it's a white tree!"

"Oh. That's cool."

"The thing is, it won't fit in my car. I need you to come pick it up?"

"What? Can't you just come home and switch cars?"

"No, I can't," I said plaintively. "It's already in the parking lot, and I can't just leave it here and I can't take it back inside." I started to cry.

Ten minutes later, Katy pulled into the parking lot. She was still wearing pajama pants, and her face looked weary and withdrawn, but she lifted most of the weight herself as we slid the box into the back of her station wagon. *So much for surprises*, I thought as she pulled away.

The next morning, I pulled Waylon's red wagon up to the back of the car and slid the box out onto it. I wheeled the box onto the back porch, opened it, and brought the layers of the tree into the house one by one. Katy and Waylon were watching an episode of *Teletubbies* that alternated documentary footage of Christmas celebrations around the world with scenes of the Tubbies trapped in a desolate, snowy winter landscape.

I studied the directions and began to assemble the tree. It took a while to understand how the different parts of the metal trunk fit together, and it took even longer to figure out how all the different sections of lights connected to the power cord. It was noon before the tree was upright and illuminated. I pulled the decorations out of the closet and unwrapped them, taking care not to hang anything breakable down low where Waylon could grab it.

By the time I finished, the winter sky was already beginning to grow dark. I made two mugs of hot chocolate, grabbed a cookie for Waylon, and turned out all the house lights. Katy propped herself up on a pile of pillows and sipped her hot chocolate.

"Isn't it a handsome tree?" I asked.

"It is," she agreed. "It's the most handsomest tree ever."

"And white trees are better than green trees," Waylon added. "Yeah!"

See, I assured myself. We're still here. We're still a family.

CHAPTER 23

Our Mother Who Art in Heaven

THE FEELING OF SECURITY was fleeting. Tuesday was Election Day, and families like ours were on the ballot.

On the drive to work, I passed a man and a woman standing at the corner of Sixth and Lamar. It was Dick and Jimmie Sue Francis, a married straight couple with a gay son. In their early sixties, with all of their kids gone from the nest, Dick and Jimmie Sue still liked to say that they were only ever as happy as their unhappiest child. They had become the official spokespeople for the campaign against the amendment, attending endless meetings in church fellowship halls and even appearing in a commercial. We all hoped that Dick's booming voice and Jimmie Sue's Texas drawl would make the anti-amendment message easier to swallow, like a glass of sweet tea.

On the morning of the election, they were holding signs urging people to vote against Prop 2. They looked so vulnerable, jumping up and down and chanting "Vote Against Hate" to apathetic commuters. It gave me a protective pang in my heart. *Please don't let it pass*, I said to no one in particular.

It passed by a three-to-one margin.

Of the 254 counties in Texas, only one voted against the amendment. The fact that it was Travis County, where we lived, was little consolation. I still felt like 75 percent of the state had spit in my face.

The day after the election, I wore black clothes to work, as if I were attending a funeral instead of meetings with faculty. As the day wore on, and everyone around me went about their business as if nothing had changed, my anger and bitterness mounted. Finally, my friend Lynda, a straight mother of three, pulled me aside.

"I just wanted to say that I'm so sorry for how things turned out," she said.

I choked back tears, sad but also immensely grateful for this sign that the straight world wasn't oblivious to the loss.

That Sunday, Gretchen asked to go to church with us. I don't think she was looking for a congregation so much as she was looking for ideas to tuck away for the day when she started her own spiritual community, one where country gospel songs rubbed shoulders with disco classics. The music at the UU church was hit or miss, and I wasn't particularly eager for an Air America-style sermon when I was feeling raw and vulnerable from the election. Katy suggested that we check out Trinity United Methodist Church. She had met the church's minister at Transgender Day of Remembrance, and she was intrigued. It seemed like an okay idea.

Trinity was nestled in a neighborhood of very modest post-WWII bungalows near the city's old airport. When I'd first moved to town, I'd read that students at a nearby elementary school actually had posttraumatic stress disorder from all the low-flying planes that swooped in and out over their homes. Perhaps as a beacon for arriving and departing aircraft, Trinity's plain white steeple was topped with a neon cross. It looked like something you'd see in Appalachia instead of Austin.

We were late arriving, but we managed to find a few seats together near the door. Instead of pews, the congregation sat in movable chairs arranged in a circle around a wooden table. It was a far cry from the raised pulpit at the UU church, and it was worlds away from the ornate altars at the Catholic churches that I had attended as a child.

Some things were familiar, though, like the recitation of the Lord's Prayer, which I refused to join. It reminded me of second grade, when I'd memorized the Ten Commandments, the Lord's Prayer and the Hail

Mary and recited them to the priest before I was allowed to make my first confession (and only then, once my childish soul was cleansed, to receive my first communion).

The drone of the Lord's Prayer made me feel like a fake. What was I doing among these people who believed in a big bearded Daddy with a kingdom in the sky? I shifted in my seat and looked down at the program. That's when I noticed an asterisk next to the word "Father."

*Feel free to substitute a name for God which resonates for you. For example: Our Mother, Creator, Great Spirit, etc.

The idea of a pagan feminist version of the Lord's Prayer made me smile and quieted some of the squirming in my soul. But then the Rev. Sid Hall—a bearded man in a short-sleeved patterned shirt—asked the congregation to offer up their prayers. I was immediately apprehensive again, not because it felt like the same pro-forma bullshit that I knew, but because it was so foreign. For someone raised in the kind of Catholic tradition that I came up in, the idea of people sharing their prayers aloud seemed positively evangelical and embarrassing. What should I expect next? Snake handlers? Speaking in tongues?

Several people asked for prayers for family members with cancer or heart problems. Some of the supplicants were explicitly political, like the elderly woman who prayed that George Bush would make better decisions, and others were achingly personal, like the soft-spoken man who had been out of work for months and was beginning to lose hope. As these strangers poured out their failures and struggles and gratitude, I felt a lump swelling in my throat. Their prayers assumed a world where suffering was a shared experience, not a moral failing or a source of shame. The pastor looked each person in the eye, repeated their prayer back to them, and then led the congregation in a common refrain: *Healing and joyful spirit, receive our prayer.*

I was tempted to add my voice to the mix—not to pray, per se—but just to say that the election had been rough, that I was feeling bruised.

But I didn't dare raise my hand. If I did, the tears welled up in my eyes would surely spill over, and I wasn't ready to cry in public. It was just a stupid marriage amendment, everyone always knew it was going to pass, and anyone with any kind of radical politics knew that marriage was a backwards way to seek equality in the first place. I focused my eyes on a crack in the plaster near the ceiling and willed my tears to stay put.

As the prayer time began to wind down, a curly-haired white woman raised her hand. "Prayers for our L-G-B-T community," she said in a careful way that made me guess she was straight. "And prayers of healing for those with fear in their hearts who voted for Prop 2."

Normally, when people said, "you're in my prayers," it seemed like a stock phrase, well meaning yet irrelevant. What difference did it make to me if they were praying to a God I didn't believe in? But this woman's prayer did make a difference. For the last five days, I'd been walking around town, looking into the faces of people who didn't care enough to vote or who voted as a slap in the face to me and my family. At best I felt invisible, at worst I felt despised. The empathy expressed in the woman's prayer soothed the fear and distrust that was festering in my own heart.

I don't remember the topic of the sermon that Sunday, nor could I tell you what songs the congregation sang. I think I was trying too hard to keep from crying. When Rev. Sid broke a loaf of bread in half and said "this table has been set for all," I couldn't hold back any more. As the congregation filled the aisles, I dug frantically through my purse, finally fishing out a crumpled tissue that was little use because the tears kept coming and every time I tried to stuff them back inside, they forced their way back out in little sobs.

In the back of the church, Katy put her arm around me, and I buried my sticky face in her shirt. I was embarrassed and a little bewildered that this gesture of unreserved hospitality could move me so deeply. For years I had believed that my half-hearted Catholic upbringing had left me bereft of faith but also relatively unscathed by spiritual violence. Now I felt fully, deeply, what my mother had meant when she suggested that communion was a symbol. Symbols were powerful. Symbols could crack your shell.

CHAPTER 24

Healing Waters

THE DAY AFTER CHRISTMAS, we boarded a plane to Florida. It was not an ideal time to be traveling, but a friend had loaned us her beach house, and I was determined to get there. I had two goals for our vacation: I wanted to fly a kite on the beach, and I wanted to start potty training Waylon.

Waylon's best friend at daycare had begun to wear underpants—or, rather, "chones," the Mexican slang word his teachers used for underwear. The more Waylon chattered about the big kids at school, lining up for "potty party" in their chones, the more I began to hope that we could leave diapers behind. Perhaps I was desperate for some sign of progress, some kind of major developmental milestone to reassure myself that our family life had not gone completely off course.

The house was on the beachfront side of a small complex. It had a porch that opened onto a marshy rectangle of grass about 20 feet from the dunes. In the morning, I laid in bed, listening to the sound of waves until the sunlight awakened Waylon and he called for his cup of milk. Katy was dead to the world, so I fed Waylon, slathered him in sunscreen, pulled on his first pair of real underpants, and headed to the beach.

At daycare, Waylon's world revolved around the sandbox—and now here he was, blessed with miles and miles of sand. We dipped our toes in the cold water and set to work digging tunnels for his trains with big pieces of shell. It was grounding to be down on all fours and covered in sand. Scoop, toss, scoop, toss, scoop. Waylon was keeping up a steady stream of chatter about trains and kids at school, whose names were often interchangeable. I tried to relax into this moment with him, but the thought of Katy lying all day in a darkened room kept pulling me backwards. I wanted her with us. It wasn't a family vacation, at least not the family vacation I'd dreamt of, unless we were all together.

After lunch, I managed to cajole Katy out onto the beach with us. She sat in a folding chair—her joints were too creaky to sit on the ground—with a beach towel wrapped around her shoulders. Her grey face matched the grey winter sky and the dull grey of the sand. She looked miserable, but at least she was miserable with us.

In order to get Waylon used to using the toilet, we had to teach him to let us know when he had to pee, so I asked him every few minutes, "Do you feel like you have to pee?" Finally he said yes, and Katy led him over to the dunes to pee into the thicket of tropical foliage. They came back looking proud.

"That's my boy," Katy said. "That's my big boy, wearing chones." She scooped him up and kissed him on the head, then released him back to his tunnels and trains.

At nap time, we had to physically remove Waylon from the beach. I sprayed his sandy legs with the hose, and then hauled him into the shower to rinse more sand from the sticky crevices of his little body. After the shower, I set him on top of the toilet and told him to try to pee again. He did, and then it was time to put a diaper back on while he slept.

"No," Waylon insisted. "I don't want that." He was over-tired and he resisted the diaper with the fury of a toddler who really, really needs a nap.

I tried to reason with him. "Waylon, we're staying at someone else's house. We can't take a risk that you might wet the bed. It's just for nap time. You can take it off as soon as you wake up."

"No, no, no, no!" he sobbed.

In the end, Katy had to hold him against her chest while I fastened the diaper and dodged his kicks. Then I laid down with him and held him until he cried himself to sleep.

By three o' clock, when Waylon was finally resting peacefully, I was exhausted. That night, after another round of beach time and sand removal and the reluctant return of the diaper, I was totally spent. I fell into bed and listened to the waves until they lulled me to sleep. I was awakened a few hours later by the sound of Katy crying out in her sleep.

"What's wrong?" I asked, sitting up suddenly.

"It's my hands," she said, with fear in her voice. "They won't stop twitching." By this time I knew better than to try to stroke her brow or kiss her face.

"Sh-sh-sh," I said. "It's okay, just breathe, baby. It's gonna be okay."

What could I do? I wasn't about to bring her more pain meds—I was already afraid to even know how much she was taking on a regular day. I couldn't call the doctor—it was after hours on December 27. Even if we managed to find him, on a cruise with his family or skiing in some mountain lodge, at best he'd only prescribe more meds with more side effects. And I couldn't begin to imagine dragging my gender-ambiguous, ex-junkie wife to the night shift at a Florida emergency room for a mystery ailment like twitching hands.

"Breathe, babe. Just breathe." She whimpered, and I drifted back to sleep.

In the morning, Waylon and I ate cereal on the patio facing the beach. A majestic blue heron swooped in and landed on the wet grass between our breakfast and the beach.

"Shh," I said to Waylon, "let's be very quiet so we don't scare her away." The giant bird regarded us for a moment and slowly sidled up to the low concrete wall surrounding the patio. She looked at us expectantly.

"I think she wants food," I marveled. I picked up a grape from Waylon's plate and tossed it into the grass. She gobbled it up and looked back at the plate.

Soon I was feeding the heron right out of my hand. Waylon was laying Cheerios on the top of the concrete barrier and then retreating to a safe distance when she came to retrieve them. It was so extraordinary to interact with this wild creature, and my first instinct was to rouse Katy so that she could experience it too, but I held back. She needed to sleep. And by the time I got her alert and out of bed, the bird would probably be gone.

Waylon and I spent the morning digging tunnels in the sand and going for "walks," which meant that he was free to run as far and as fast as he could along the deserted winter beach, and I hurried to keep him in my sights. I was so tired that even a slow jog left me winded, and I sometimes had to yell, "Stop, *stop!*" in order to catch up with my little man running wild in his brand new briefs.

When we returned to the house, Katy was gone. She'd left a note saying that she'd gone into town for groceries. I suspected that she was headed to the health food store that we'd passed on the way in from the airport, and I just hoped that she wouldn't come back with more Himalayan crystal salt.

As I showered the sand off of Waylon and cajoled him into bed for his nap, my chest was tight and tears hovered just behind my eyes. I was angry at being left alone, angry at all the responsibilities I had to shoulder, and angry at the bitterness that was creeping into my time with Waylon. But who could I be mad at, really? Finding no conceivable outlet for the rage that was building inside me, my brain and body shifted gears. I drifted off to sleep beside Waylon in a state of numbness.

Katy returned from the health food store with a bottle of papaya enzyme pills. She was full of her conversations with the sages of the supplement aisle, which I pointedly ignored. I was busy arranging watercolor sets and cups of water on the table on the back porch. If Katy couldn't come out to the beach for family time, then family time would come to her. If she insisted on seeking out questionable New Age cures, I was equally insistent that we were going to act like a family, dammit, and we were going to do things together as a family.

The early evening sky was a spectacular display of orange and purple and blue. In the distance we could see the silhouettes of stick-legged sea birds darting in and out of the tide. Katy took to the watercolors immediately, saturating sheet after sheet with the brilliant colors of the sunset. Waylon was on his knees in the deck chair next to her. Holding his brush in his little fist with immense concentration, he pulled it in a long line across the textured watercolor paper. At the end of the line, he stopped, dipped his brush in paint, and added a second, shorter line at a 45-degree angle from the first. He repeated the same shape several times on different paintings.

"What are you painting, Buddy?" I had never seen him make anything besides a tangled mess of scribbles before.

"It's a bird," he said matter-of-factly.

His first representational painting! *I will remember this moment*, I told myself, and it seemed I could see my life as two diverging lines, one moving uphill, toward milestones and progress, the other sliding downward, toward dissolution and death.

That night, I fell into bed, exhausted again. Several hours later, I was awakened by the sound of Katy moving around our room. As I surfaced from sleep, I realized that she was rummaging through the dresser drawers. "What are you doing?" I asked.

"I thought I saw some medical tape in here." Again I could hear the sound of fear in her voice.

"What? Why?"

"My fingers are seizing up. They won't stop spasming. I have to tape them together."

I hoped that she was sleepwalking. I hoped that she was dreaming on some combination of sleeping pills and pain meds. It seemed incumbent on me to take charge of the situation, to put her back in bed or call an ambulance, or whatever the sane course of action might be. But I couldn't. I was paralyzed, pinned to the bed by the sheer effort of trying not to panic. I drifted out of the moment and back into sleep.

When I woke in the morning, I hoped for a few seconds that it had all been a bad dream, but I rolled over to find Katy's fingers wrapped in tape like a mummy, the plastic tape dispenser still trailing from her right hand. I bounded out of bed and shuttled Waylon off to eat bagels on the beach. I thought, at the time, that I was shielding him from a disturbing scene, but I realize now that I was really protecting myself. I was convinced that Katy was dying—if not from the toxic interferon treatments, then from the OxyContin that reduced her to a grim relic of her former self.

On New Year's Day, the weather turned grey and cold. I insisted on bundling Waylon in his yellow fleece jacket and taking him out to the beach to fly a kite. Once I launched the fragile plastic toy into the air, the winter winds tossed it hither and yon. It didn't matter. As I ran down the beach with the spool unfurling in my hand, I felt infinitely more control than I did over the zigzag path of my life. Katy ambled out to the beach in her pajama pants to watch, and I knew she was trying to support me with the one thing she had to give: her presence. Waylon, intimidated by the hefty tug of the kite string, clamored for Katy to pick him up. When the wind died down and the sun began to set over the ocean, I snapped a picture of the two of them cheek to cheek. *Remember this.*

Part III

Brian sings with Waylon at the Rokitt reunion

Waylon with Donna, a few months before she entered the hospital.

CHAPTER 25

Sleep with My Wife, Please

When we returned from our trip to the beach, I was more exhausted than ever. I no longer had the energy to guard my privacy or pretend that I had things under control. We needed help. We needed witnesses. We needed saner and more rested minds to help us navigate the next rough patch. But asking for help impinged on Katy's privacy as well, and I felt obliged to ask her permission to proceed. I waited until we were at the therapist's office, in case I needed back up.

"I really need to get a few solid nights of sleep," I ventured.

Katy bristled at the other end of the couch, like a porcupine that protectively puffs out his quills. I could imagine what she was thinking. *Oh yeah, you think* you're *not sleeping well? I'm the one who wakes up howling in pain!*

"I was wondering if..." *Say it. Say it.* "I was wondering if we could ask a few of your friends to come spend the night with you. That way I could sleep in the guest room for a couple of nights and just, you know, recharge my batteries."

Claire cocked one eyebrow at Katy, expectantly. Katy was staring out the window just above my head. She didn't say anything at first, and my heart was in my throat, but then she nodded. "Yeah, that could work. That sounds like a good idea."

I was flooded with relief and anxiety at the same time. It's awkward to ask your friends to sleep with your wife. I was afraid that everyone would say, *Oh, you know, I would be glad to help, but I have to get up so darn early for work. Can I bring you a casserole instead?* In fact, my fear of rejection was only slightly less intense than my fear of going on alone. I was grateful when Katy offered to make the actual requests. I suspected that it was easier for her to ask for help on my behalf. "Paige really needs a break," was less embarrassing than "I can't get out of bed on my own anymore."

Katy called three friends—Dianne, Nancy, and Rachael—and they all said yes right away. I can't remember who took the first turn, but I remember lying in the guest bedroom, listening vigilantly for sounds from upstairs. All was quiet. *Oh my God, we're like the boy who cried wolf. We're going to use up all their generosity and then something worse will happen, and everyone will think that we're just drama queens, and there won't be anyone left to call.* I couldn't relax into the loving hands of friends, because some old part of my brain kept insisting that I was wrong to ask for help. *Now our friends will see the mountains of unfolded laundry and the bedside table stacked with pills. They'll see the medical waste containers overflowing with used needles and the vacant way that Katy stares at the television. They'll see the all the videos that Waylon watches in the morning because his parents are too tired to play.*

To interrupt this flood of judgments, I forced myself to think about prayer time at Trinity United Methodist. Every Sunday, people stood in the circle and talked about getting fired from their jobs or not being able to find jobs. People told the whole congregation about wrecking their cars or wrestling with addictions. It didn't make them seem like big losers. It just made them seem human.

One Sunday morning, a homeless vet had wandered into Trinity. When Rev. Sid asked for the prayers of the people, the man rose and thanked God for marijuana and LSD. No one batted an eye. The man went on. He asked God for forgiveness, because marijuana and LSD had kept him from his true calling, which was the anti-war movement. I looked around the small sanctuary, with its cracked and crumbling walls. No one looked ashamed or uncomfortable for this man who wore his contradictions on his dirty sleeve. No one seemed to think he wasn't deserving of help just because he was a mess.

"Healing and joyful spirit," Sid intoned.

"Receive our prayer," the congregation answered.

I forced myself to meditate on the kind, unembarrassed faces of the people who listened to the prayers. I fell asleep trying to imagine our family through their eyes.

In the morning, I awoke to the sound of Waylon playing hide-and-seek upstairs with one of his beloved aunties. I checked the clock and noted that I'd slept seven hours—the longest uninterrupted sleep I'd had in months. I rested my head back on the pillow and luxuriated in the rays of sunlight peeking through the guestroom blinds. I still felt unworthy and embarrassed. But I also felt loved, rested, and a little more ready to deal with whatever came next.

CHAPTER 26

Going to the Desert

SHORTLY AFTER NEW YEAR'S, Katy went to see her liver doctor. It had been nine months since she started treatment, although it felt like much longer. After the appointment, she called me at the office.

"What did he say?"

"My viral load is up," she said, her voice heavy with defeat. "Way up."

I felt a familiar icy hand squeezing my heart. "What does he want to do?" I couldn't even imagine what punishment was in store.

"I told him no more. I can't do this anymore."

The hand wrenched my heart again and then let go. I was terrified to imagine what this meant for our future, but I was relieved to think that there might be some kind of reprieve, however temporary.

"I support you, no matter what you decide to do."

"I'm sorry."

"There's nothing to be sorry for," I said, bursting into tears.

When we hung up, I sat in my swivel chair and stared at the wall. All the suffering. All the terror and loneliness and fighting. It had all been for nothing.

Everything was different. Everything was the same. The little rituals of daily life rolled on: sippy cup, school, work, dinner, bath, story, song. Waylon never wanted to say goodnight. In the final moments before sleep, he excavated his deepest fears, dredging up urgent questions designed to keep Katy at his side for a little longer.

"Can a bulldozer break down the side of our house?"

"What if a robber steals all my toys?"

"Are you and Mama going to die before me?"

The first time I heard this question, the blood turned to ice water in my veins. *It's my fault. He knows what I'm thinking.* I tried to shake it off, to pretend it was just a fleeting phase, but Waylon was insistent. Soon the questions weren't confined to bedtime. I'd be driving him home from school or fixing dinner when it would start. "Why do we have to die? Will we be together when we die?"

"None of us is going to die for a long time," I'd say, going for the pat but hopefully comforting answer. "Have some macaroni and cheese." He never fell for it.

"But *when* are you going to die? I want to die the same time as you," he'd say. His sense of autobiographical time was fairly limited, so reassuring him that we'd be around until he was an adult was almost like saying we were going to abandon him next week.

I was convinced that we had done this to him, with our gloomy home full of pills and syringes and anxiety. Katy tried to soothe me with therapist speak, explaining that a tiny obsession with one's parents' death was a normal part of separation and individuation. I found some comfort in these words, but I knew she was more concerned than she let on. At bedtime, she and Waylon began to spend longer and longer chatting in the dark. I'd pass by the bedroom door and hear odd fragments of unfamiliar terms, like "etheric realm" and "astral body." I knew just enough to understand that she was drawing on her old junkie knowledge, all the metaphysical books she'd read with the strobe-light intensity of crystal meth consciousness. Now she was refashioning them into a parental toolkit for nighttime angst.

I seriously doubted that a young child could comprehend such arcane terminology. However, if it gave him some comfort, if it provided some ladder to transcend his fears, then I didn't think it could hurt.

Katy called me at work a few weeks later, out of breath.

"I just had breakfast with Alan, and his new girlfriend's ex-boyfriend had hep C. He was really far along, he had cirrhosis, he was dying. They found out about this doctor in New Mexico, he treats hep C patients with infusions of alpha lipoic acid. She had to practically carry him on the plane. They didn't think he was going to make it, but he got there, and the doctor treated him, and it saved his life. She said it was like a miracle."

"Oh. Wow." Her words wafted into my ear, vibrated across my delicately tuned skeptical faculties, and made sounds like this: "Desperation went to New Mexico and then quackery, plus snake oil. Gullible, bullshit, New Age hooey."

In our marriage, Katy had always been responsible for believing in miracles, the afterlife, and alternative medicine. I was in charge of doubting and demanding empirical evidence. But now I was convinced she was dying. I thought she deserved to do it her way. Also, I knew she *would* do it her way, no matter what I said. It seemed better to indulge her than to mar our precious time together.

"Uh, that sounds really interesting."

That night, Katy ordered all of the doctor's books on the Internet. Although I was trying to remain neutral, I did have a few protective impulses. I peeked at her Amazon account and was surprised to see that Dr. Burt Berkson's books had been published by reputable publishing houses. Meanwhile, Katy immersed herself in patient forums, where people with all kinds of chronic illnesses testified that Berkson had saved their lives in scenarios every bit as dramatic as the one we'd heard from Alan's girlfriend. Katy quoted from these testimonials at length. They seemed too good to be true, but I didn't say so. I limited myself to a quick search of the doctor's credentials. He had a PhD in Biology, as well as an MD. Some of his research seemed to have been published in peer-reviewed journals. *Maybe it won't be the worst kind of snake oil.*

In a matter of days, Katy had an appointment at Berkson's clinic in Las Cruces, New Mexico. Before I even had time to wrap my head around the whole thing, she was getting blood work done in preparation for her consultation. "What's your viral load?" I asked, bracing myself for the answer.

"Dr. Berkson doesn't look at viral load," she replied. "He says viral load is irrelevant as long as your liver enzymes are normal." *Quack, quack, kah-quack, quack*, said my skeptical faculties.

In March, a little over a year after Katy had begun interferon treatment, she flew to El Paso and rented a car. For the next five days, she reported to the Integrative Medical Clinic of New Mexico twice a day for hour-long intravenous infusions of alpha lipoic acid. By the time Waylon and I arrived midweek, she had bruises up and down both arms.

"I told 'em not to use that vein," she said knowingly, pointing at a black and blue spot on her forearm. "It looks like a big fatty, but *that* vein will roll."

Fifteen minutes into our visit, I came down with the kind of sinus infection that sucks you into a black hole of despair. I spent 72 hours dozing in the dark, low-ceilinged room of the Best Western motor court. While Katy was at the clinic, Waylon sat beside me in the bed, watching a marathon of *Teenage Mutant Ninja Turtles* cartoons. I could practically hear his little brain atrophying from the relentless repetition of the turtles' theme song: "Heroes in a half shell—turtle power!"

I was powerless to get out of bed and find something better for him to do, so I sank back down into a decongestant fog. *Please let me get better,* I prayed to no one in particular.

On Friday, I managed to rally enough to accompany Katy to her meeting with Dr. Berkson. The clinic was just off the freeway in an understated adobe office complex. I was pleasantly surprised to see that the waiting room seemed professional. I don't know what I had expected—Incense? Wind chimes? This just seemed like an ordinary doctor's office, except there was no television blaring Fox news in the waiting room, and the atmosphere seemed hopeful rather than resigned. There were no toys of course, none of those infernal wire structures with brightly colored wooden beads, because few people brought a child along for the ride on their last-ditch attempt at survival. Waylon wandered in the direction of an emaciated woman with a purple scarf tied around her hairless head. I worried that he might cause her some chagrin with his round cheeks, his blonde curls, and his undeniable aliveness. But the woman smiled at him serenely.

"She could hardly walk when she got here," Katy whispered. "Pancreatic cancer."

A nurse called us back to the doctor's consulting office. We passed the infusion room, where I glimpsed walls lined on both sides with reclining chairs and IV poles. Several patients were seated there, arms attached to plastic tubes that were dripping solutions into their veins. Further down, Dr. Berkson's office door was ajar. When we entered the book-lined chamber, a stocky, bearded man rose from behind the desk and shook my hand, not flinching or looking puzzled when Katy introduced me as her wife and Waylon as our son. His grasp was firm and no-nonsense. He looked and acted not-at-all like the tanned, white-toothed charlatan that I'd imagined. On his desk was a dossier full of Katy's blood work, and he immediately launched into discussion of Katy's albumin levels and other indicators of liver health.

"The liver has the capacity to heal itself," Dr. Berkson explained. I knew this, vaguely, from the myth of Prometheus, who is chained to Mt. Caucasus for the crime of stealing fire. Every day, "the winged hound of Zeus, the ravening eagle" arrives and rips poor Prometheus's liver to shreds. Every night, the unrepentant Titan's liver regenerates, and the cycle begins again the next day. My mother told me this story when I was a little girl, and I had always been horrified by the dread and anticipation that Prometheus must have felt when the sun rose each morning and he waited for the eagle to descend again. I was so horrified, in fact, that I missed a crucial point: the eagle doesn't kill Prometheus.

We had tried heroic measures, tried to banish the virus from Katy's blood for good. It didn't work and nearly killed her. Now, it seemed to me, Dr. Berkson was offering Katy the option of learning to live in balance with the virus. We weren't going to erase the specter of death on the horizon, but rather hold it close, like a wrestler who clinches his opponent to forestall a final blow.

When I tuned back into the conversation, Dr. Berkson was giving lifestyle advice: Eat lots of whole grains and vegetables. Avoid processed foods. Take your vitamins. Avoid stress. All of these things seemed eminently reasonable. He asked if we had any more questions, and then, in his business-like manner, he was done. We gathered Waylon and found our way to the waiting room.

"Wait, so what's the next step?" I asked Katy, still a little light-headed from cold medicine.

"Now we wait for my new blood work to come back," Katy said. "To see if I'm responding."

I was neither hopeful nor unhopeful. I thought of the visit to the desert as something that had to be gotten through. We'd all survived it, Dr. Berkson hadn't been as bad as I'd feared, and I'd managed to avoid a conflict with Katy. This fundamental divide—the distance between materialism and mysticism—was a danger zone in our marriage, a minefield I'd learned to traverse rarely and carefully ever since our first visit to Lily Dale. Despite the Promethean possibilities that I'd glimpsed in the doctor's office, I wasn't waiting with baited breath for Katy's lab results. In fact, when she called me a few days later at the office, it took me a minute to remember what she was talking about.

"Myenzymesaredown!"

"Slow down. What are you saying?"

"My liver enzymes. They're back in normal range! They were so jacked up, sky high, and now they're back within normal range. They haven't been like this since I got diagnosed with hep C!"

I confess that I did not immediately join in her rejoicing. I felt protective, and I did not want to give way to wanton hope when I had paid so dearly for the clear-eyed acceptance of Katy's imminent demise. It was weeks, maybe even months, before I allowed myself to admit that she might not be dying. Or rather, she was always dying, but the end might not come any time soon.

One evening, I was driving Waylon home from day care. The time in the car, just the two of us, was one of my favorite periods of the day. We had some of our best conversations when he was buckled in his car seat, describing the minor dramas of the playground. On this particular day, however, I had launched into a kind of therapeutic monologue.

"Mommy doesn't feel good right now, but it's not your fault that she can't play," I said. Katy had been stricken with a bad bout of arthritis that morning, and I had read that kids tend to blame themselves when a parent is incapacitated. "She wants to play with you very much. She loves you so much."

I wanted to tell him that she was going to get better, that everything was going to be okay, but I didn't know if that was true. "It won't always be like it is right now," was the best I could do

"Mama?"

"What?" I was expecting a heart-wrenching revelation about his feelings of abandonment.

"Do you think I might be *your* parent in the next life?"

There was laughter in his voice; the idea of a role reversal was clearly amusing.

"Yes," I allowed, smiling back at him in the rearview mirror. "It's possible." I was astounded that he was still pondering Katy's teachings on reincarnation. Here I was, mired in the problems of the present and bracing for terrible losses in the not-to-distant future. But in Waylon's mind, the bonds between us were so strong that they transcended this earthly time and place. I felt like a weight had been lifted from my heart. Between daycare and the dinner table, I experienced a moment of pure joy.

CHAPTER 27

Drag Showdown

IN THE WEEKS THAT followed, things changed, but not as much as you might think. Gone were the Thursday night shots and the weekly bouts of nausea and dizziness. The bruises on Katy's belly had healed, and she no longer had to drink a gallon of water every day, which meant she slept a little better at night. But the pain in her joints was unabated, she was still taking painkillers, still fatigued and distant.

One night, she came home from work with more energy than usual. She was all atwitter about a drag competition at an old gay bar called Charlie's. She started pulling boxes out of the coat closet and pawing through them.

"I know my old Bette Midler costume is in here somewhere," she said, tossing clothes willy-nilly on the floor. In the mid-eighties, Katy had lived in Palm Springs. By day she ran a steak house called Katy's Yellow Rose. At night, fueled by crystal meth, she performed on the Southern California club circuit in lip sync competitions sponsored by the television show *Puttin' on the Hits*. Bette Midler's "When a Man Loves a Woman" had been her signature song.

"Aha!" she exclaimed, pulling a rumpled women's evening jacket from the pile.

"Wait—is this a drag king thing, or a drag queen thing?"

"I dunno. It doesn't say."

I was full of questions, but Katy was already on the phone, calling everyone she knew. Listening in on the conversations, I learned that Katy planned on performing "When a Man Loves a Woman," and she wanted a full fake backup band. Like the pied piper of lesbians, she was enticing local performance artists and seasoned musicians to pick up toy drums and plastic trombones. In the past, Katy's ability to bring queer people together to put on a show had been one of the things I loved most. At the moment, however, I failed to appreciate this particular charm.

For the next several days, our living space was awash with feathers and glitter and hot glue guns. Saturday morning, as Katy put the finishing touches on her costume, I loaded Waylon into the stroller for a walk around the lake. I needed to burn off some energy. I was seething. *She finally feels better, and this is what she does? Fuck her. Fuck her. Fuck her.* I walked faster and faster, glad that Waylon couldn't see my face. I wanted to get the rage out of me, to be able to celebrate the fact that Katy was back among the living, but I couldn't, because I still felt like I was parenting alone.

The competition was hosted by the United Court of Austin, a drag queen community that typically did not have much truck with folks assigned female at birth. When our little crew of punk rock dykes with toy instruments strolled in, I could feel the crowd assessing our comfortable shoes.

Katy had asked me to document the evening, so I was walking around behind a video camera, which suited my removed, ironic attitude just fine. I certainly didn't want to get up and act goofy on stage with our friends. *Look at them,* I thought, panning the crowd. *They're probably so happy that Katy's back. They don't know what this is going to cost her. They don't know what it is going to cost me.*

When it was Katy's turn to perform, she walked out to the canned applause of the soundtrack from *The Rose,* fluffing the blonde curly strands of her wig and gesturing with a maroon feather boa.

"You know, sometimes people say to me, Rose, when's the first time you ever heard the blues?" Katy knew the monologue by heart; she hit every syllable flawlessly. "And you know what I tell them? I tell them the day I was born. You know why? You know why? Because I was born a woman!" The queens were eating it up, hooting and hollering, giving her the perfect set-up for the next line. "Ah! Oh! We got some noisy females in the house tonight!"

It had been so long since I'd seen Katy perform. I'd forgotten how charismatic she could be on stage. I was completely captivated until she got to the part of the song about the lengths a man will go to when he loves a woman. "He can't keep his mind on nothing else, he'll trade the world for the good thing he found." I wanted to feel like she was singing about me, about us, but I knew perfectly well that it wasn't true.

When the music stopped, Katy pulled off her wig, old-school drag style. She yanked down the tunic and pulled the stuffing out of the shiny, peach-colored bra that she'd purchased for the occasion.

Katy was pumped up after her performance, and her ebullience grew when they announced the performers who were advancing to the next round. She flitted around the club, bestowing appreciations on her "band," and then disappearing to the back for a costume change. I stood at the side of the stage and fiddled with the camera settings, too sad to talk or join in the general merriment.

The second round of the competition was a fashion show. The other competitors sashayed out in evening gowns and cocktail dresses, took a turn on the imaginary catwalk, displayed their flawless accessories, and then tiptoed out on their platform heels. When it was Katy's turn again, she strutted out in motorcycle boots, spiky hair, white pants, and a tight black shirt that highlighted her man-chest. If it hadn't been for the hooting and hollering of our friends, you probably could've heard a pin drop. The judges looked at each other and then back at the stage. In the previous round, they'd assumed she was a drag queen, but now she was competing in boy drag, which wasn't really even a category in this particular competition. There was a great deal of conferring, and Katy's second-round score was noticeably lower than the previous round.

In the end, I think Katy received some kind of honorable mention. I felt proud, and protective, but not terribly surprised. Still high from her performance, Katy was incredulous, outraged, full of piss and vinegar, until we came home and she collapsed into bed, exhausted. She stayed there for the rest of the weekend, leaving me to clean up the feathers and the glitter and the piles of discarded clothes.

I was still seething two days later when we met up at our therapist's office. I just barely managed to contain my anger until we reached the safety of the couch.

"It just feels like as soon as she feels a little bit better…," I explained, haltingly, "as soon as she has energy, she's spending it on something else. There's no trade-off, because when she's done performing, there's nothing left." I felt like I had been saying the same things for months. I was always angry, always feeling like Katy took too much.

Katy was hunched at the far end of the couch hugging a lumpy chenille pillow. Claire looked grim. She started to say something, then seemed to think better of it, then forged ahead.

"You're always concentrating on trying to get Katy to take up less space in your relationship," she said. "What if you put that same energy into trying to take up more space yourself? It's possible that, if you started claiming your space—instead of waiting for Katy to give it to you—the relationship might come into better balance."

My stomach dropped like I was rolling down the steep side of a rollercoaster. All my life, I'd been waiting for permission—from my parents, my professors, and from Katy. It was stifling but safe. As long as other people had the power, my desires remained conditional and my failures rested on someone else—this is what I *would* do, if only my parents didn't have expectations, if only Waylon didn't need me, if only Katy weren't so selfish. Now Claire was calling me out, asking me to figure out what I wanted to do, and then just do it, consequences be damned.

Hot tears blurred my eyes. A lump swelled in my throat. I felt exposed, like a bug wriggling under a microscope. Beneath all the complaints about Katy's selfishness, beneath all the bitterness about how the illness had taken over my life, there was a fear of naming the things I wanted and actually pursuing them on my own.

Claire didn't just have words for me. Perhaps we'd been stuck in the same place for so long that we had actually driven her to be blunt about facts she'd only hinted at before. She told Katy frankly that her behavior at the drag show sounded manic. Katy hugged the pillow closer, and I could tell she felt like a bug under a microscope too, but Claire didn't stop. She explained that manic behavior could be a defense mechanism, a way to distract oneself from an unbearable reality.

"Your body has been failing you, you haven't been able to do all of the things you used to. You've been extremely dependent on Paige these last several months. It's scary to need someone else that much. You've been in a dark place."

Katy nodded her head. I thought about how galling it must have been for her to ask me for help getting out of bed all those nights.

Claire continued. "It's natural that you would want some escape, that you would want to feel powerful, like you've triumphed over your weakness." Katy nodded again. I felt relieved that someone else had recognized and named this behavior. I wasn't crazy. I wasn't just jealous of Katy's creativity or clinging to my victim role. Now that the manic defense had a name, it seemed it would be easier to recognize and actually talk about.

"The key is just to notice your behavior. You don't have to judge," Claire said to both of us. "Just try to be curious about what's under there."

For my therapy homework, I was supposed to practice acting as entitled and taking up as much space as Katy. This sounded fine in theory, but I had no idea how to move from theory to practice. How was I supposed to just start doing the things that I'd been avoiding for years?

The answer—or at least the first step toward an answer—arrived in the mail. It was a course catalogue from The Crossings, a Buddhist retreat center in the Texas hill country just outside of Austin. I was flipping through it one morning while I ate my breakfast cereal, and I noticed that one of my favorite writers was coming to town to teach a weeklong workshop. *Wow*, I thought. *I'd love to do that. If only Katy wasn't sick and Waylon wasn't so young.*

It was the "if only" that tipped me off. I hit the pause button on the familiar litany of excuses and forced myself to rewind. A week alone at a writing retreat? It sounded so good. I craved the solitude and the opportunity for sustained, uninterrupted creativity like a starving person craves food. But what about the other people at the retreat? Would I fit in? Would I feel socially awkward? What if I sucked at writing? It was tempting to dwell on all the logistical details rather than face these fears. Could we afford it? Who would pick Waylon up from school if I was gone for a week? Who would start dinner? What if Katy didn't feel good? What if Waylon missed me too much?

Even as I considered these practical obstacles, I knew that I was psyching myself out. If Katy were in the same situation, she wouldn't stay home. She would schedule a babysitter. I forced myself to move forward the way I thought that she would. If I was going to take up space, I might as well learn from the best.

"Lynda Barry is coming to teach a week-long workshop at The Crossings," I told Katy that night as we were climbing into bed.

"That's cool."

"I want to do it." There. I said it.

"How many days is it?" I assumed that her question was loaded with incredulity and opposition, but I forced myself to answer as though it were merely an informational question.

"It's five full days, Monday through Friday."

"How much does it cost?"

Oh! It was agony to withstand this inquisition.

"It's $1,500, which I know is a lot, but I have some research money that I need to spend at work. I think I can use it."

"Who's going to pick up Waylon?"

I was almost ready to give up. This resistance was too much for me. "I'm going to get a babysitter," I said with my last burst of strength.

"Okay, it sounds like you've got it all figured out," she said, leaning over to kiss me goodnight. "I'll miss you."

Katy drifted off to sleep. I lay awake and wondered. Had the disapproval that I detected been real or imagined? It almost didn't matter, I realized, because I'd persevered. The sky hadn't fallen. Katy hadn't broken up with me or accused me of being a selfish bitch. She might have felt mildly inconvenienced, but I'd stuck to my guns and she'd adjusted, just like Claire said that she would.

The workshop was amazing. I wrote thousands of words just for myself, for the sheer joy of making sense of my experiences. It was also awkward at times, like summer camp for grownups. Sometimes I missed Katy and Waylon, but I slept soundly in my tiny dormitory-style bed. In the late afternoons, I hiked aimlessly into the hill country, just tuning in to the sound of my own inner dialogue. It was during one of these walks that I realized that I hated my job. Or rather, I loved the teaching but hated the administrative part that required me to accept my place in the university hierarchy. It was time, I knew, to take up more space at work too. I just had to find the right opportunity.

CHAPTER 28

⁂

No Shortage

A COUPLE OF WEEKS later, I was checking my email when I noticed a message from an activist I'd met during the No Nonsense in November campaign. Jeff Lutes had recently become the Executive Director of Soulforce, a national LGBT social justice organization, and now he was looking to hire a Director of National Media.

The title sounded great, but there were a few small problems. First, I'd never worked in media relations before. I had only a vague idea of what a media director might do, but I figured all my years of teaching entry-level rhetoric courses might allow me to fake it.

Second, despite the lofty title, Director of National Media was a part-time job with no benefits. I had a full-time job with health insurance and a pension plan. Surely it would be madness to trade financial security for an uncertain future as an activist, right?

Finally, there was a question of cultural differences. Soulforce was founded by Mel White, a Christian evangelical minister and erstwhile ghostwriter for the likes of Jerry Falwell. After coming out as gay and being ostracized by his former employers and brothers in Christ, Mel had devoted his life to stopping spiritual violence against LGBT people. Inspired by Gandhi and King, White taught the philosophy of nonviolence and the tactics of civil disobedience to call attention to the hypocrisy of Christian churches that excluded gays and lesbians or sent them to soul-killing "ex-gay" therapy.

All of this sounded great to me, but Soulforce's most devoted supporters tended to be LGBT people who had experienced profound spiritual violence in Christian churches. Many of them hailed from evangelical traditions. They were about as different from my feminist, sex-positive, gender-non-conforming community as it was possible for queers to be.

"It's crazy, right?" I said to Katy. "I'm probably not even qualified. And how could I take a part-time job?"

"I think you should just go for it. Let the universe sort out the details." I almost forgot to roll my eyes when Katy invoked the mystical powers of the universe.

A week later, I was sitting in a cafe with Jeff. With his starched khaki pants and brilliant white polo shirt, Jeff could slip into a Baptist worship service on any given Sunday, his sculpted biceps and perfectly polished bald head legible only to the queens in the choir. The fact that Jeff could come across as the nice Southern Baptist boy was one of the reasons he'd been tapped to fill the Executive Director role when Mel stepped down from day-to-day leadership at Soulforce. The other reason was his track record. The previous summer, Jeff had organized more than a thousand Soulforce supporters to participate in a direct action at the headquarters of Focus on the Family, the powerful Christian think tank that promoted straight, white, patriarchal "family values" and funded ex-gay therapies. The action made national news and even forced Focus on the Family to shut its doors for the day in order to avoid encounters with nontraditional families.

Jeff and I hit it off immediately. We're both born organizers, happiest when we're brainstorming and planning, and it felt very natural to feed off of each other's energy. I was touched by what he told me about the suffering of LGBT people raised in exclusionary churches, and I was drawn to Soulforce's methods of direct action—marches, sit-ins, die-ins and more. After a year of feeling ineffectual, I was ready to dive in and make a difference.

Still, when Jeff offered me the job, I was beside myself. Only a few months before, Katy had been barely working. My salary at the university was not extravagant, but it was more dependable than the income from Katy's therapy practice, which tended to rise and fall with the seasons and her health. Soulforce was a tiny organization, its payroll largely dependent on the whims of individual donors. At the university I worked regular hours. At Soulforce, I'd work long, irregular hours, with lots of travel, and I'd always be on call in case of a media emergency.

"I just don't think I can do that to you and Waylon," I told Katy. I knew it was the responsible thing to say. "I don't see how we can afford it."

"I don't see how we can afford for you *not* to do it," Katy countered. "You're miserable in your job right now. That's not good for any of us."

"I know, it's just..."

"Look, they're going to love you. Pretty soon they'll realize that you're indispensable and hire you full time. If they don't, you can pick up some teaching or something."

"Yeah, maybe." I didn't want to be overly optimistic about my prospects, but I was starting to feel pretty excited.

"My being sick has taken up a lot of room in our life this past year. It's your turn."

I couldn't believe what I was hearing. Katy's illness had grown and grown until I felt like Alice in Wonderland with my ear pushed up against the chimney—only instead of me growing larger and larger, I felt like our life was growing smaller and smaller. The idea that it was my "turn," that Katy and I might wax and wane to accommodate one another, was profoundly healing.

A few weeks later, I was working the phones for Soulforce. We were collaborating on a project with an LGBT-affirming black church in Dallas, and I had to tell the church's outreach director that I wouldn't be able to drive up for our first in-person planning session because it coincided with Waylon's third birthday.

"Oh no. You can't miss your baby's birthday. Jesus will be mad at you."

"Uh..." I wasn't sure what to say.

"Jesus. Will. Be. Mad. At. You." She was very emphatic.

"Well, I definitely wouldn't want that," I said, steering the conversation back to how many sandwiches to order for the meeting.

When the call ended, I paused for a moment before returning to my laptop and my insistent queue of unanswered emails. What would it be like to have faith like that? To feel it in your heart and bones, without a doubt as to Jesus's opinions on birthday parties and other matters of personal significance? I felt like a perennial outsider to belief, alternately fascinated and repelled by its certainties. The more closely I observed it, the more mystified I became by its mechanisms. How did it happen? Were some people just born with it? If not, how did it get inside of you?

One afternoon, I arrived at daycare to find Waylon sitting by himself on the playground with a faraway look in his eyes. This in itself was unusual. Waylon was usually surrounded by other kids and talking a blue streak about trains and sand and the endless tunnel networks they constructed out of sections of PVC pipe. Today he barely seemed to hear me when I greeted him. He was lost in his own world, like a person in a state of shock.

I started to panic. Visions of 1980s satanic daycare hysteria reared their heads. I gathered up Waylon's things and led him quickly to the car. It was only in the parking lot, when I was helping him into his seat, that he seemed to tune into my presence.

"Mom," he said, in the tiniest, most frightened voice. "Pee was coming out of my butt!"

Diarrhea. In all our many parenting manuals, no expert had ever suggested that we warn Waylon about diarrhea. He even didn't know it was a thing!

Physically, Waylon recovered quickly, but his nerves took longer to settle than his stomach. Two weeks later, we were playing with trains in the living room.

"I have to poop right now," he said, jumping to his feet. "Or else I'm gonna poop in my pants."

"We don't want that to happen," I said, scrambling to follow him.

"No, we don't," Waylon said, shaking his head gravely.

I could tell he was remembering the diarrhea incident, and I wanted to make sure he wasn't feeling any shame about it. I sat down on the side of the tub. "But sometimes you can't help it, like when you have diarrhea. No one can help pooping in their pants if they have bad diarrhea."

"Jesus could," Waylon grunted from the toilet.

"Hmmm," I said distractedly. I was still thinking about whether Waylon had poop trauma. "I don't know, he was supposed to be just a regular man."

"Well, if he could walk on water, why couldn't he stop diarrhea?" Waylon asked impatiently.

I had to laugh. "That's a very good question. I don't know."

I couldn't wait to tell my friends about how Waylon pondered Jesus's poop. But the more I repeated the anecdote, the more it weighed on me. I hadn't even been aware that Waylon knew the story of Jesus walking on water! Clearly, his mind was like a sponge, soaking up everything he heard and trying to make sense of it through the lens of his own experiences. As a parent, I was supposed to be guiding him, but I felt like an aimless wanderer in the world of faith. It reminded me of walking up and down the streets of Lily Dale, teetering between doubt and belief. Now that Waylon was growing older, I felt renewed pressure to pick a side.

It might seem like working for Soulforce would be the ideal way to sort through my spiritual ambivalence, but I was usually a few steps removed from the work on the ground. The Media Director's job was to write press releases, organize media events and get reporters interested in covering our direct actions. My outsider perspective actually came in handy when I dealt with mainstream media, because I knew exactly which details of evangelical culture would titillate them. However, on the rare occasions when I was involved in the face-to-face dialogue work, I was afraid of being exposed as a lapsed Catholic who knew little of the Bible, a poser who attended an ultra-liberal Methodist church with a special 9 a.m. service for pagans. People at Trinity tended to say that they were "on a faith journey." Language like that would not cut the mustard with folks who believed that the Bible was the literal word of God.

Paradoxically, the self-contained nature of evangelical culture made it easier to fake my way through. The people I met at Christian colleges and churches tended to assume that everyone valued the same things they valued. Yes, I might be queer, and, yes, I might be under the mistaken impression that my abomination was somehow pleasing to Jesus—but it never seemed to occur to them that I might not care one way or the other about Jesus's good opinion.

The LGBT Christians who were drawn to Soulforce were more diverse. Many were survivors of ex-gay ministries that had taught them to suspect every impulse, to distrust and disavow their bodies. They had emerged transformed, but not necessarily in the manner the ex-gay leaders had hoped. Some had lost their faith altogether, and others had become extremely suspicious of religious authority. A significant subset managed to find a measure of self-acceptance while keeping the rest of their religious beliefs intact.

At one point, Soulforce invited a former ex-gay minister from England to address a gathering of fellow ex-gay survivors. This man had been a spokesperson for Exodus International, the world's largest association of ex-gay ministries, but he had discovered, to his dismay, that he couldn't eradicate his homosexual leanings through prayer or penance. Now he led a kind of support group for other men who were struggling to reconcile gay identities with evangelical beliefs.

I suppose I thought that a British evangelical would be fundamentally different from his American counterparts, more sophisticated and urbane. After the public meeting, some of my fellow organizers and I took him to dinner. I invited along my grad-school friend Alyssa, a secular Jew who had taught a workshop for allies as part of the day's events. Halfway through dinner, the middle-aged Brit eyed her with curiosity.

"Why are you wearing a star of Solomon?" he asked, nodding at her necklace.

Alyssa looked taken aback, and I was aghast. In my world, one assumed that a person wearing a simple six-pointed star was expressing some form of Jewish identity.

"It's a star of David," Alyssa said awkwardly. The Brit continued to look at her expectantly. "I wear it because my family is Jewish." I felt protective of Alyssa, who had, at my request, entered into this world that seemed to expect straightforward professions of faith.

The man looked unconvinced. There was something inside him, some imperturbable certainty, that didn't jibe with what she was saying. Perhaps he wanted to argue that it really was a star of Solomon. Or perhaps he couldn't believe that a perfectly nice Jew could spend all day with Christians and still resist the awesome power of Jesus.

I had been working with Soulforce for several months when I got a text from Jeff. "Someone just outed Ted Haggard!!!!"

I hastened to my computer to find out who in the heck Ted Haggard was before a reporter called me for a comment. A quick search revealed that Haggard was the pastor of a thriving mega-church, the president of the 30-million-member National Association of Evangelicals, and a frequent advisor to the White House. As a Colorado resident, Haggard had been outspoken in his support for Amendment 43, an anti-gay-marriage amendment similar to Prop 2 in Texas. Now, just a few days before the election, a male prostitute named Mike Jones had come forward to allege that Haggard had been paying him for sex and crystal meth.

Initially, some of Haggard's evangelical cronies supported him, but as the story grew legs and Haggard reluctantly acknowledged that at least some parts of the allegations were true, they quickly began to distance themselves. Suddenly Pat Robertson and Jerry Falwell were very vague on their past association with Haggard, and the White House downplayed Haggard's role in its weekly calls with faith leaders. In a few days, Haggard resigned from the leadership of the National Association of Evangelicals, and he was fired from his position at New Life Church. In a letter of apology to the congregation, Haggard wrote, "There is a part of my life that is so repulsive and dark that I have been warring against it all of my adult life." The elders of the church remanded him to emergency counseling with a secretive group of evangelical leaders who promised to use a variety of methods—including polygraph tests and laying on of hands—to try to restore Haggard to the straight and narrow.

In the secular world, Haggard became a laughingstock. His crisis was a kind of shorthand for the idea that the most virulently anti-gay leaders were driven by their own struggles with homosexual impulses. His name became synonymous with hypocrisy, and his past media appearances, in which he had cultivated a robust-yet-smarmy American masculinity, now seemed mannered and hilarious, as if he were a lesser-known minister character in the Village People.

It was hard not to indulge in schadenfreude, especially after living through the Prop 2 campaign in Texas the year before. Even though Colorado's anti-gay amendment passed with 56 percent of the vote, I still felt a tiny bit vindicated that one of the law's main supporters had been exposed. I was happily recording an *Anderson Cooper 360°* segment on the scandal when Jeff called.

"I was thinking about a nonviolent response to Ted Haggard's situation."

I wiped the smug smile off my face. "Oh, uh-huh."

"He's lost his job, his congregation, possibly even his family. Now they're sending him to reparative therapy. This is an opportunity to reach out to him in empathy. We should ask members of the LGBT community to write him letters of compassion and concern."

Uh, Jeff, I hate to break it to you, but I don't think that queer people are feeling too compassionate toward old Ted right now. I think they're happy that a hater is getting a taste of his own medicine.

"Oooookay," I said, keeping my real thoughts to myself.

I was afraid that Soulforce would look naive. Jeff argued that many LGBT people, especially LGBT Christians, had lost everything when they came out or were outed. If they were able to connect with Haggard, he would experience our community in a new light. This was an opportunity to help him through a difficult time, maybe even save him from becoming an ex-gay poster boy whom the religious right would trot out to prove that their destructive and discredited "cures" really worked—until the cure didn't work, at which point they would abandon him all over again.

The letter project seemed like a long shot, but nonviolent direct action was all about long shots. I dutifully wrote a press release asking people to write to Haggard in care of Soulforce. The release inspired many news stories and blog posts. Most writers were incredulous that an LGBT organization would urge compassion for someone who had been so vocally anti-gay.

When the letters began to pour into the Soulforce website, Jeff and I divided the labor. He used his contacts to try to find out how to reach Haggard, who had been swept off to an undisclosed location. My job was to print out each of the messages and seal them in individual envelopes. I read as I worked, stopping every once in a while to wipe away tears.

The letters said, "I've been where you are. I was a pastor, or a youth minister or a successful business owner." They said, "I lost my family, my job, my congregation, my friends. I was so humiliated and ashamed. I prayed for God to change me. I hated myself and I wanted to die." Almost without fail, the authors wanted to tell Haggard that he was stronger than he thought, that he would survive. They quoted his own words about the "dark and repulsive" part of himself and assured him that he was a beloved child of God and deserved to walk in the light.

The letters were so fucking generous. I was used to thinking of my forgiveness as a precious commodity. These LGBT Christians acted like they had an unlimited supply of forgiveness and love! For everyone—even Ted Haggard.

A few days before Christmas, I was printing and mailing the last few letters to Ted. I put on my new mix CD, a holiday gift that Gretchen had made from her extensive collection of corny gospel LPs. As usual, it was difficult to tell if Gretchen's enthusiasm was earnest or ironic. I fully expected the CD to be aurally challenging. To my surprise, I immediately fell in love with one of the songs. It was a Tammy Faye Bakker disco number called "No Shortage," a glorious specimen of seventies camp that warned of coming shortages on gas, coal oil, meat, wheat, and even glass. At the end of each swelling chorus, Tammy Faye reminded listeners that "there's no shortage on God's mercy, there's no shortage of God's love!"

The peppy synthesized brass riff got stuck in my head and made me want to make jazz hands. The concept of "mercy" had come alive for me, and I was in the mood to celebrate. I don't know if the letters ever reached Ted Haggard, or whether they moved him, but they definitely changed me. After months of bitterness and rage, the dried-up well of my compassion was restored. I was flooded with forgiveness and generosity. In the wake of all the shame and loneliness I'd felt when Katy was sick, it was wonderful to realize that failure and suffering could sometimes become a powerful source of connection and caring.

The longer I worked for Soulforce, the more opportunities I had to spend with social-justice oriented Christians. The way these people talked about (and lived) the presence of God in their lives was real and compelling. When we marched or stood vigil together, I had a hint of what a conversion experience might feel like. I was in awe of their purpose and unity. At the same time, I was uncomfortably aware of how quickly things became Christian-centric whenever two or more were gathered in His name. When we collaborated with other organizations, I cringed to think about the activists who were not Christians and how quickly and easily some Soulforcers shifted into talking as if everyone believed the same thing.

Born-again Christians often talk about when they "met Jesus," as if Jesus just walked up to them in the supermarket. When I worked for Soulforce, I met a lot of great people, but I never met Jesus. And that was fine. After all, I had taken the job to do justice, not to be born again. But I felt a pang of responsibility toward Waylon. My parents had given me such a mixed bag of religious messages. I wished that I had something more vivid and coherent to pass down to my son.

One afternoon, Waylon was engaged in an art project of his own devising, which involved gluing a bunch of sequins to a cork. As he was working at the kitchen table, I heard him singing a little song that went "God is inside of every thing, God is inside of everything, God is inside of everything!" The melody sounded a lot like the Ramones, but the lyrics gave me pause.

"Who taught you that song? Did you learn that in Sunday school?" I asked. I realized I had no clear idea what he learned when he attended the children's activities at Trinity.

"No one taught it to me. I taught it to myself."

"Oh, okay. That's good." I picked up a few stray sequins and put them back in his pile.

"Mom," he said, still gluing.

"Yes?"

"God is inside of this table."

I smiled and watched him finish his project. I was excited to see what it would become. I knew Waylon would find his own way through the mysteries of faith. I didn't have to figure everything out—not for him, and not for myself either.

CHAPTER 29

❧

Donor Duet

TWO DAYS BEFORE BRIAN was due to arrive in Texas, Katy walked in the door with a bulging plastic trash bag full of secondhand toys.

I shook my head. "Waylon already has too many toys. His birthday was a month ago! He's barely four and he has enough stuff to fill two closets."

"I know, I know," she replied, looking sheepish. "But he's going to be the only kid at the beach this weekend."

This was one of our most familiar family dynamics: Katy indulged, Paige worried, Waylon got the loot. But for once I wasn't fretting about my son's consumer character. I was more concerned about my wife's impulse to play Santa in July.

On the surface, her justification for the new toys was entirely plausible. We were about to embark on the kind of trip down memory lane that only the middle-aged can appreciate. Waylon's sperm donor was coming to Texas to play a reunion show with Rokitt, his hair metal band from the late eighties. But rather than the gritty Texas blues clubs that they played in their prime, this time Rokitt was planning to electrify their die-hard fans from the fluorescently lit comfort of the Stahlman Park Recreation Center at Surfside Beach, a tiny village south of Galveston.

Surfside Beach is not exactly the Riviera of the Texas coast. But Waylon wasn't exactly a beach snob. He played in the sand all day long at preschool, digging holes and tunnels and rivers. Every night, at bath time, he was reluctantly parted from a personal reserve of sand. Despite Katy's worries, there could be no doubt that he was looking forward to a vacation that involved beaches full of unlimited sand.

It wasn't clear, however, whether Waylon was looking forward to seeing "Uncle" Brian. They had only met once, when Waylon was about eighteen months old, and I knew Waylon didn't remember. Brian called him at Christmas and birthday time, and Waylon communicated with the harassed politeness that children everywhere extend to long-distance relatives.

With the Rokitt reunion on the horizon, Katy had been pulling out old pictures and trying to enlist Waylon's enthusiasm for the band and its sperm donor front man.

"Waylon," she said, holding out a picture from an amateur photo shoot circa 1987, "do you know who this is?"

Waylon looked up from his blocks, scanned the picture of a man in ripped tank top and lace tights, and shook his head.

"That's Uncle Brian!" Katy explained, in a singsong Barney voice. "Remember, he gave us the seed that we needed to make you?"

This line about the seed was what we'd been telling Waylon ever since he was old enough for us to tell him something about the way we made him. I worried at times that it was too euphemistic, but it was *technically* accurate. Thus far, although Waylon loved to hear stories about how his parents met and decided to have a baby, he hadn't expressed interest in the mechanics of conception. From what I could tell, it hadn't yet crossed his radar that two people with ovaries couldn't make a baby on their own. Whatever we were saying about seeds just seemed extraneous.

Regardless of what Waylon understood, Katy's enthusiasm for her best friend and his band was hard to resist. Over the last few days, Waylon had begun to recognize the guy in the pictures and to look forward to seeing Rokitt play. I was getting excited, too. But I was also scared.

Brian wasn't part of our queer milieu of chosen family. He had a wife, an ex-wife, and a son in high school. The few times that we'd met, I hadn't been able to decipher his dudely, understated manners. From my vantage point, it wasn't clear if Brian was really down for new and complicated family ties. I feared that this vacation would set Waylon up to expect a relationship that would never materialize.

When I wasn't fretting about too little connection, I worried about too much connection. I imagined Waylon, fifteen and leather-jacketed, leaving home in a storm of adolescent angst.

"You just don't understand me," he yelled as the backdoor slammed shut. "I'm going to live with my Dad." Dad. Dad. Dad. In fantasy, the forbidden D-word lingered in the air as Katy and I huddled in the kitchen, broken apron strings dangling limply at our sides. What if Waylon and Brian had some kind of mystical masculine bond? What if Waylon decided to abandon his moms? Could Brian love and support our son without trying to supplant us? Was Katy secretly worried about this too? Was that the real explanation for her toy store shopping spree?

All of these worries were swirling in my mind when Waylon came home from preschool and gravitated to the big bag of toys. Katy told him he could pick one now and save the rest for the beach, so he closed his eyes and plunged his hand into the bag, feeling around until he located the largest toy: a three-foot plastic robot with a helmet and a ray gun. (Apparently my feminist, nonviolent shopping criteria were the first casualty of Brian's visit.) Waylon was in heaven. Grinning, he searched for the "on" switch. And then there was sound:

"I-am-Master," the robot announced. "I-sense-your-fear."

Before Waylon was born, I believed that my future child would not watch much television. On the rare occasions when he did watch television, I imagined, it would be something that *I* liked—something witty and subversive like *PeeWee's Playhouse*. Apparently there's a karmic debt to be paid for such hubris, because my son turned out to like television, quite a bit. At age four, his favorite show was still *Thomas and Friends*, a neo-Victorian boy's tale about anthropomorphic steam engines who compete to be "a really useful engine" in the eyes of pig-eyed industrialist called Sir Topham Hatt.

"Mom, can I watch just one more *Thomas*?" Waylon asked, his face so contorted with exaggerated yearning that I couldn't begrudge a few more minutes of vegging out. We had spent the morning jumping waves and building sand castles and flying kites on the beach. We were exhausted and a little bit sunburned. We'd had a late lunch and a shower, I'd removed most of the sand from Waylon's hair, and now we were lounging on the worn couch of our rented beach house. We were waiting for Katy and Brian to return from band practice.

"Okay," I said, cuddling him closer. "You can watch one more episode. But you have to turn it off when Uncle Brian gets back."

Two days earlier, when Brian and his wife Kathy arrived at our house in Austin, Waylon had dutifully dispensed hugs and kisses before retreating to the safety of his toys. Today was our first full day at the beach, and Waylon was still a little shy around the newcomers.

I remembered what it was like to meet some relative whom your parents always talked about. You felt pressure to produce fond feelings, to fall in love with this new person. But it was awkward, even stifling, because the relationship was pre-defined. I was thinking about how to help Waylon feel comfortable (and succumbing to a familiar *Thomas and Friends* stupor), when I heard the sound of boots on the outside stairs. Katy came in first, walked over, kissed us both, and sat on the couch. Brian entered next, nodded in our general direction, and headed to the fridge for a beer.

Over the past 24 hours, Brian had become increasingly edgy and withdrawn. Today's practice was the first of only three full rehearsals for the show. Some of the band members hadn't touched their instruments for almost twenty years. From the look on Brian's face, I guessed things hadn't gone so well.

He brought his beer into the living room and sat across from us, looking pale beneath his five o' clock shadow. He looked like a different man from the rocker in Katy's old photos. His long, bleached hair was now short and dark. He wore cargo shorts and a baggy t-shirt. It was hard to believe that he'd once pranced around the stage in eyeliner and a jockstrap. Right now he looked like he'd prefer to crawl under a blanket and never come out.

"Waylon," I said, "it's time to turn off Thomas." I was afraid that the perky voices of the steam engines would push Brian over the edge.

For once, Waylon turned off the TV without complaining. While Katy and I chatted about band practice, he dragged Master the robot from behind the couch and began to play in Brian's vicinity. I could see Waylon looking at this new grown-up from the corner of his eye. I guessed that he wanted to engage, but he wasn't quite sure how to begin. He flipped Master's switch on and off, over and over again.

"I-am-Master. I-sense-your-fear."

"I-am-Master. I-sense-your-fear."

"I-am…"

"Wait," Brian said, coming out of his reverie, "what is he saying?"

Waylon repeated it for him slowly, "He says 'I sense your fear.'"

"No," Brian said, deadpan. "No." Waylon looked confused, almost heartbroken.

"No," Brian explained, "he says, 'I-am-Master. I'll-buy-you-a-beer.'"

Waylon cracked up. Apparently this was one of the funniest things he'd ever heard. He couldn't stop repeating it, talking over Master's mechanical voice, forcing the robot to buy endless rounds of cheer for everyone in the living room.

Surfside Beach is connected to the mainland by a string of chemical plants. Vast plantations of pipes and cooling towers squat over the shallow waters of the bay. At night, illuminated by security lights, the plants seem strangely beautiful. In the daytime, they conjure visions of tumors and three-headed fish.

We were traversing this no man's land because Katy had a mission. She had found an old picture of Brian onstage, naked except for a cigarette, a fedora, and a strategically placed guitar. We were driving to the Brazosport Mall to get it transferred onto t-shirts for the show.

"I want a shirt too," Waylon said from the back. "I want a shirt with Uncle Brian on it."

"Hmm," I said. "I'm not sure that would be appropriate."

"Oh, what the hell," Katy protested. "He wants a t-shirt of his donor."

"Well, you can't wear it to school," I said, weakly. What the hell. It *was* a hilarious picture.

We were just coming over the bridge to the mainland, and Katy pulled over at a store called Buc-cee's, which was a combination convenience store, surf shop, and t-shirt emporium. They sold diesel fuel, bikinis, flip flops, and blow-up rafts, along with hamburgers, chicken wings, chewing tobacco, beer, and homemade fig preserves.

Waylon was immediately drawn to a large display of sand pails and shovels. Katy headed for the children's clothes and started flipping through the racks for a size 4 black t-shirt. I decided to try on floppy sun hats. If you can't beat the consumers, I figured, you might as well get something good.

"Mommy, Mommy, can I have this?"

Waylon was dragging an enormous plastic ship through the racks of bathing suits and trunks. When it was clear that he was addressing Katy as "Mommy," everyone in the store, from the teenage girl in the bikini aisle to the trucker waiting for his food order, did a double take. I couldn't tell if Katy noticed.

"Sure," she said automatically. "Check out this t-shirt." She held up a black t-shirt with an anchor on the sleeve that said "Surfside Beach." It matched the tattoos on her arms.

"Yes!" Waylon exclaimed. They high-fived.

The line at the cash register was long. One vacationing family was buying snacks for a day on Surfside. But mostly it was chemical plant workers, grabbing coffee and donuts before reporting to shifts at Dow and Shintech. Katy scooped up Waylon and held him while we waited.

"My boy," she said, kissing his head. "My boy is going to get a shirt just like Mommy's." Waylon nodded enthusiastically. "If anybody asks you who's on the back, what do you say?"

Waylon shrugged.

"You say, 'that's my *donor!*'"

That night, after practice, Brian was even more nervous. He sat silently through dinner, answering his wife's cheerful queries about band practice with terse, one-word answers. Kathy's daughter Jessica was visiting from college, and I felt bad, because Brian's nerves were casting a pall over their mother-daughter time.

"We could build a bonfire on the beach tonight?" Kathy asked, hopefully. Brian shrugged and stared at his food. The silence was awkward, unbearable. All of the women, myself included, immediately began to fill it with airy small talk. But when Brian left the room, Kathy scraped his plate with barely contained fury, her lips pressed together in a thin line. After the dishes were done, she wiped the Formica table in sharp, precise circles.

I hovered between helping and not helping. The whole scene was like a rerun of the family gatherings of my early adolescence. I knew the script by heart: men set the mood, women set the table. As a teenager, I'd vowed to resist my assigned role in this drama. Now, stuck in the beach house, I felt angsty and oddly irritated with Katy. *I didn't sign on for this much heterosexuality! Why are you making me sit through this?* I wanted to hold my hands over Waylon's eyes. *Don't watch!*

My angst was tempered by a guilty sense of sympathy. I guessed Kathy wasn't used to seeing her husband this nervous. They had met long after he retired from Rokitt. In her world, Brian was a caseworker at an agency for people with developmental disabilities. I had seen him with some of his clients when we visited Michigan. He was relaxed, patient, sweet.

After dinner, Brian retired to the back porch to smoke. Everyone else gathered in the living room. It was clear that no bonfire was going to materialize.

"Mom, can I watch one more Thomas?" Waylon asked.

I felt ambivalent. I knew he was bored, but I didn't want to be rude, hogging the TV with kiddie shows.

"Ask Uncle Brian if he wants to use the TV," I answered. Just then, Brian walked in the door and started to cross the room. Waylon followed him across the linoleum floor.

"Can I watch TV?" he asked, tugging on Brian's shorts.

"I don't know," Brian said, sullenly. His whole body recoiled from the responsibility that the question implied. "Ask your mom."

The next day, Waylon and I escaped to the beach to jump waves. Every few minutes he yelled, "This is so fun!" as if he couldn't quite believe his luck. I felt the same way. As a child, I would stay in the surf for so long that my body could feel the rise and fall of the waves in my bed at night. Now Waylon's excitement was making me feel like we shared a special bond.

When he got winded, I held him on my hip and jumped for him. Waylon told me stories about preschool. I told him stories about childhood vacations. We talked until I ran out of stories, but he still wasn't ready to go ashore.

"Are you excited for the big rock show tonight?" I asked.

"Uh-huh." He shook his head. We'd been taking him to shows since he was a month old.

"Are you going to dance for Uncle Brian?" I asked.

"Yes, and I'm going to sing with the band. On the stage." he informed me.

"Oh." This was the first time I'd heard of this plan. I didn't want to smash his dreams, but I also didn't want him to be disappointed if it didn't work out.

"Um, Sweetie, *Mommy* is singing with the band. Did anyone tell you that you were going to sing with the band?"

"No," he said serenely. "I just am."

The sun was setting on the beach as we made our way down Surfside's narrow, two-lane highway. When we pulled up to the Stahlman Park Recreation Center, I was relieved to see that the parking area was fairly crowded. It helped that every third vehicle was a puffed-up Ford F150, which takes up one and a half regular parking spaces.

I released Waylon from the back of our Volkswagen. He looked adorable in his black t-shirt. "Are you ready to rock?" I asked.

"Yeah!" he yelled.

"We're going to dance and clap really loud, right?"

"Yeah, and I'm going to sing with Uncle Brian," he assured me as we walked across the sandy parking lot.

"That's a sweet idea," I told him, taking his hand. "But it's not very likely, at least not tonight." I knew that I sounded like a wet blanket. I just didn't want my baby to get hurt. Waylon broke away and charged up the wooden ramp to the rec center. The outdoor floodlights illuminated the picture of Brian on his back.

"Slow down!" I yelled as he disappeared through the swinging doors.

The danger of any kind of reunion is finding out that you're just not that relevant to people's lives. I had only heard about Rokitt from Katy, and she was Brian's best friend. I didn't have my own sense of what Rokitt meant to other folks—until I walked into the bright, air-conditioned space of the rec center. The folding chairs were filled with old rockers and their teenage kids, chatting and eating in tidy rows of 10-foot banquet tables. I spotted Waylon near the kitchen, where a team of women was setting out cookies. The buffet table was decorated like a high school prom, with plastic picture cubes that displayed Rokitt photos on all six sides.

By the time I made it across the room, Waylon had a cookie in hand and was making his escape. He ran straight into his Tía Sandra, another of Katy's former roommates, who caught him in a bear hug. As I made my way to where they were standing, Sandra pretended to devour the "sugars" from Waylon's neck, which made him laugh and squeal. When she finally handed him back to me, he was content to rest on my hip and eat his cookie for a few minutes.

"Sandra," I asked, "did you know Brian when he was in Rokitt?" Sandra and I are the same age—nearly a decade younger than most of the people in the rec hall—and I was curious to hear her perspective on the whole scene.

"I went to see them when I was in high school. Some of my rocker friends took me to their show at the KC hall. The next day, everyone was wearing Rokitt t-shirts to class. You would have thought fuckin' Motley Crue had come to town."

I had seen pictures of Sandra from the eighties, when her black, curly hair was styled in a glorious Mexican mullet. Back then, she and Katy were both identified as "butches with hair." Now she wore it close to her head in a crew cut. She had recently been hired as an operator at one of the plants that lined the beach road, and she was the proud owner of a big, puffy F-150 in the parking lot.

A white man with hands and neck like sunburned hams was approaching. *Redneck alert! Redneck alert!* I pulled Waylon closer to me. As the ham man walked past, on his way to the cookie tray, he gave Sandra a subtle nod. "How you doing?" Sandra said, nodding back. I marveled at how my friend found her place in a world of men who work in the volatile chemical plants.

Suddenly, the band members took their places. There was no stage, so they just walked, unceremoniously, to their instruments. A skinny guy with hair like Kenny G spoke into the microphone. I guessed that he was the emcee, but the people in the audience just ignored him. Brian was pacing in front of the drum kit, his movements cramped by nervousness. He was wearing Katy's tight black jeans and a t-shirt that said "I rock," with a picture of an antique rocking chair. His face was deathly pale. I was afraid he might puke before the end of the introduction. Finally, the emcee handed over the mic. The band started to play. Brian let out a feeble whoop. The audience finally stopped talking.

In the back of the room, I was holding my breath. *Please don't let them suck,* I said to the universe. But they actually sounded okay. Brian's voice was clear and tuneful. He was stiff, but he managed a jaunty kick at the end of the first song. *Whew!* I moved to an empty folding chair near Kathy. Waylon scooted onto my lap as the band dove into their second number, a Judas Priest cover. I snuck a peek at Kathy's face. She looked happy and relieved and a little teary. Rokitt was loosening up now, and the crowd showered them with hearty applause. In the next row, a little old lady with white hair turned to her daughter. "Breakin' the law, breakin' the law," she sang spryly.

Brian was starting to look less frightened. "I just took some Geritol, and I'm waiting for it to kick in," he joked between songs. I wondered if anyone under 35 had ever heard of Geritol.

"Feel free to dance, if you can find some room," he added. "Any time."

I'm from Austin, where there's an unspoken thirteenth commandment: thou shalt dance when thy friend's band plays. At the Stahlman Park Recreational Center, the folding chairs dominated all but a tiny space in the very front. People were behaving like they were at a church social—grabbing plates of potato salad and catching up with their neighbors while the band played. Between the chatter and the bright lights and the absence of an actual stage, the whole thing was lacking a certain intensity. I worried about the energy of Brian and the other guys. I just wanted people in this room to bear proper witness to the miracle of middle-aged men making music together.

Katy tried to move up to the front to dance, but she was interrupted every few minutes by someone who wanted to catch up on old times. Katy was elected "Howdy Queen" at her high school, an honor bestowed on the friendliest freshman girl. However, even as Howdy Queen, Katy didn't look like a girl. I've seen the coronation photos; she looked like a football player with falsies and a prom dress. Twenty-five years later, she had a surgically flattened chest and could wear her clothing of choice: jeans and a muscle shirt. Her body was still ambiguous. And her warmth and enthusiasm still had the power to charm people who would otherwise be frightened by the mystery.

It didn't hurt that she was the daughter of a football coach. When Katy walked up to sing with Brian, the little old lady in the front whispered something to her daughter. I imagined it was along the lines of "Who's that dyke?" Her daughter answered and the lady shook her head excitedly. "Oh, that's Katy Koonce." She tapped her husband on the shoulder. "That's Katy Koonce!" she yelled in his ear. He shook his head too. Perhaps he was remembering the year when Brazoswood High won the state football championship. Katy ran onto the field with her dad after every game.

Now the hometown crew cheered as Katy humped Brian's leg through the chorus of "Talk Dirty to Me." It was hard to believe that the Stahlman Park Recreation Center was bearing witness to such a queer spectacle. The two old friends fed each other's energy, and their duet shifted the mood in the room. Donna Koonce, who had been holding court by the back door, lifted the hem of her skirt and broke into her signature dance, pointing her toe and pumping her skinny legs like a Rockette.

Waylon was out of his seat and dancing too. As the band made its way through original numbers like "Sweet Sixteen" and "You Make Love Too Tough," he bounced and banged his head. Occasionally he threw in some kung fu moves and King Tut poses. Every time he got too close to the band, I had to run up in front of the folding chairs and drag him out of the spotlight. "That's Katy Koonce's lesbian lover," I imagined the old woman saying to her husband. "And their gay love child!"

After the tenth time that Waylon rushed the band, I pulled him aside for a little talk.

"Mommy was singing with the band because they invited her," I explained. "You can't keep going up there and getting in their way. It's Uncle Brian's big night."

Waylon nodded obediently and then ran away. An old friend of Katy's stopped to talk to me, but I was distracted, trying to spot Waylon in the crowd. By the time my eyes found him, he was already back at the front. He had somehow managed to take apart one of the plastic picture cubes, and he was holding a handful of old photos. As the band launched into the final song, Waylon crawled up to the microphone and carefully laid the pictures at Brian's feet.

"You show us everything you've got," Brian growled into the mic. "And baby, baby that's quite a lot."

Waylon was jumping up an down, elated. He loved this song! Brian leaned down toward him for the chorus.

"I wanna rock and roll all night," Brian growled.

He extended the microphone to Waylon. Waylon contemplated it for a beat.

"And party ev-er-y day!" he squealed in his high, four-year-old voice.

Brian lead into the chorus again, and Waylon sang his part. He was on the beat now, and people in the room were beginning to laugh and look at one another like, "Who is that kid?" By the time the second chorus came around, the two fell into an easy call and response: first phrase low and gravelly, second phrase high and squeaky.

"I wanna rock and roll all night," Brian called.

"And party ev-e-ry day!" Waylon answered, looking proud. Every time he hit his line, people in the crowd hooted and clapped. It was a magical moment, the kind that I wished would never end because I couldn't quite believe it was real.

Katy came up and put her arms around me. I could feel her tears sliding down my neck. I looked around the room and saw Sandra against the back wall. She was smiling and crying big butch tears too. Sandra had helped raise two nieces in this community. Now she and her girlfriend were thinking about having a baby of their own.

Brian nodded to the band to play the chorus one more time. "I wanna rock and roll all night!"

"And party every day!" They sang the last line together. Brian hung up his microphone and swept Waylon into his arms. Waylon threw his arms around Brian's neck, and they hugged for a long time. Brian turned to the audience and made the devil horns. Waylon painstakingly folded his middle fingers down to imitate Brian's heavy metal salute.

The crowd was shouting and clapping and calling for an encore. They were honoring Rokitt and honoring their youth. It felt like they were honoring our queer family, with all of its twists and unexpected turns. Despite my fears and reservations, I was so glad that we had chosen Brian as our donor, so very glad that we had made room in our lives for more love.

CHAPTER 30

─────── ⤜⧉⤛ ───────

Boygirls and Girlboys

SIX MONTHS LATER, WAYLON and I were working in the garden when he captured a pill bug. The poor creature had curled up into a little protective ball, and Waylon was about to shove it in his pocket, but then thought better of it.

"Mom, I put that roly poly in the plant, and he or she—or if it's a girlboy or a boygirl—is going to dig in the dirt and make it soft."

As a feminist parent, I have experienced few greater joys than hearing non-sexist language carefully applied to a pill bug. But although I would love to take credit for Waylon's refusal to assume the gender of the bug, it was really his own creative adaptation to his context, just as "girlboy" and "boygirl" were categories he created to describe the people around him.

When I was in college, my psychology professor taught that children begin to consolidate their concepts of gender identity around three years of age, and that the process is often marked by heightened rigidity about gender norms. So I thoroughly expected Waylon to become a little gender cop. He *did* go through a phase when he wanted to categorize everyone. One of his favorite games was a toddler form of people watching, where he would look at people in the park or in the grocery store and yell out "boy!" or "girl!" And while I wanted to support Waylon in whatever developmental thing he was working through, this game could be extremely socially mortifying. I would estimate that he was "right" (in that his attributions matched the gender identities of passersby) about 70 percent of the time.

Luckily it didn't take Waylon too long to come up against the inadequacy of his binary categories. Another of his favorite games around this time was to ask, over and over, "Mama, are you a girl?" For me it was fairly easy to answer with a straightforward, "Yes." But for Katy, things were not so simple. Since he asked this question about ten times a day for at least a month, she had plenty of time to formulate a good answer.

"I'm kind of a mix of girl and boy," she'd say. "I'm a mommy, but I look more like a boy than Mama does."

Waylon did not skip a beat. Before long, he was asking "Mommy, are you a boygirl?" ten times a day, and Waylon's four-coordinate gender axis (girl, boy, boygirl, girlboy) was born. It wasn't exhaustive (what gender system could be?), but it had a little more descriptive depth than a binary.

At Christmas time, we decided to splurge and spend a few nights at a fancy beach resort. From the moment the clerk ushered us into the "VIP check-in room," I knew we were in for an adventure. Waylon plunged head first into a butter-colored club chair.

"Honey, please keep your shoes off the furniture," I said, feeling my class insecurities creep up like a slow and annoying blush.

"But, Mama, I'm a seal." He rested his front flippers on the marble floor.

I scanned the clerk's face, hoping for the knowing look that tells you you're in the presence of Family. Nary a blip on the old gaydar. His eyes were resolutely glued to his computer screen.

Katy was not helping. Early that morning, she'd loaded up our vacation baggage. Then she'd navigated the car through hectic holiday traffic. Now she slouched in the chair beside me, tattooed arms folded across her pecs, head tilted back in a caricature of repose. Mirrored sunglasses shielded her eyes. She was ready for a nap.

I gamely answered the check-in questions, keeping one eye on Waylon, who was maneuvering across the floor on his belly. Like his parents, he was clad in black. His t-shirt was emblazoned with an electric guitar and the words "Toxic Waste." I wondered what the clerk thought of our tousled entourage. Perhaps he thought that only the truly rich and famous would be bold enough to despoil the Sand Pearl Resort with such dishevelment. *Did he think we might be rock stars?*

Apparently, he sized us up and designated us "Mr. and Mrs. Schilt." As in, "Well, Mr. and Mrs. Schilt, we hope you enjoy your stay."

"The bellman will get those bags, Mr. Schilt."

"Can I get you some ice, Mrs. Schilt?"

Thus registered in the hotel's central database, we seemed doomed to pass the remainder of our holiday as hapless characters in a comedy of errors.

Back when Waylon was three years old, we had begun trying to include him in the ritual of holiday gift giving. "Waylon," I began, "what do you think Mommy would like for Christmas?"

"Trains," he said, without missing a beat.

"What do you think Grandma would like?" I persisted.

"Trains."

"What do you think we should get for Auntie?" By this time I was just testing.

"Trains."

By the following Christmas, gift giving was still largely an exercise. With lots of not-so-subtle encouragement from his parents, Waylon strung some necklaces for friends and family, but he hadn't really developed the capacity to imagine another person's needs and desires. Most of his handiwork looked like a random aggregation of begrudgingly selected shapes and colors.

Ironically, the one bright glimmer of hope was the necklace Waylon made for my sister, an old-school goth with a penchant for black tights, ripped crinolines and creepy Victorian bonnets. When he sat down to make Auntie's necklace, Waylon carefully selected the darkest and most macabre beads in his little craft kit. Heartened, I consulted my childrearing bible, a tattered copy of *Touchpoints*, which reassured me that empathy—the capacity to imagine another person's needs and feelings—develops along a slow and uneven trajectory.

One day, not long after Waylon made his aunt a gothic necklace, Katy and I were stretched out on the beige couch in Claire's beige office. We were talking about parenting (our favorite "easy" topic), and I happened to mention some of Waylon's ideas about gender.

Claire's normally unflappable exterior betrayed a hint of concern. As her eyebrow arched upward, I moved defensively to the edge of the couch. She asked a follow-up question. And then another.

"We've always talked about my surgery," Katy explained. "He knows that I never felt completely like a girl and that I changed my chest to be more comfortable in my body."

"He has his own vocabulary," I added. "He calls Katy a 'boy-girl.'"

Claire seemed most concerned about whether Waylon believed that his own gender and sex might be malleable. According to psychoanalytic timetables, core gender identity is supposed to be consolidated by two or three years of age. Were Claire's pursed lips suggesting that we were in danger of derailing our child's development? Did she secretly believe, like folks on the religious right, that queer parenting was an irresponsible social experiment?

Part of me felt defiant, wanting to challenge the whole notion of static gender identity. Another (irrational) part of me was sure she was going to call Child Protective Services the moment we left her office.

Queer people have been told for so long that we are not fit to be parents. It's impossible not to internalize some of the shame that is projected onto us, especially when it comes to our culture's most hallowed idol, the family. So I felt the sting of Claire's troubled look. But I also understood that her reaction was rooted in the assumption that what's normal is natural and good.

As queer parents, our gift is to remember all the coaxing, coercion, and even outright violence it takes to make normal gender development seem inevitable and desirable. By the logic of that trajectory, we did not turn out okay—yet we know that we turned out okay. If we can hold onto this contradiction, if we can resist the shame, we can forge new family values that affirm gender diversity as a precious gift.

Just before our trip to the beach resort, we went to Target to find a gift for Waylon's friend Laila. As we crossed the crowded parking lot, I asked Waylon what he thought Laila would like, fully expecting him to list his latest vehicular obsessions.

"Umm, I think ... Barbie."

Has ever a parenting moment been more bittersweet? I hugged him and showered him with praise for thinking about someone else's feelings.

Privately, I was imagining my white, blonde, blue-eyed son delivering a Barbie to his brown-skinned, black-haired girlfriend. It looked like a tableau with the caption "Gender and Imperialism."

Luckily, at that moment, Katy caught up with us and settled the matter with a quick phone call to Laila's mom. It turned out that Waylon was right; Laila was expecting a Barbie Dream House from Santa. And she needed furniture. Relieved that we would not bear the responsibility of introducing our young friend to Barbie, I followed my family to the toy aisle, where we proceeded to ponder tiny pink bedroom sets.

A few days later, we were installed at the fancy beach resort. It was beginning to dawn on me that two hundred dollars a night buys an alarmingly frequent level of personal contact. The entire staff seemed to be connected by walkie-talkie; as we passed from reception to the lobby to our room, we were repeatedly greeted as "Mr. and Mrs. Schilt."

Although her identity is somewhere between genders, Katy is quite content to pass as male in such situations. It's her voice that usually gives her away. That evening, in the time it took for the waiter to unpack our room service order, she had gone from "Mr. Schilt" to "ma'am." We joked about it on the way home, imagining a one-woman show called "From Mister to Ma'am."

Not to be left out of the joke, Waylon said, "Yeah, he didn't realize that you were a girl-boy," in a tone of comic exasperation.

"Wait, I thought you called Mommy a 'boy-girl,'" I said.

"No, that was back when I was only thinking of myself, so I always put 'boy' first. But now I'm thinking of other people," he explained.

Sitting in the front seat, I felt my heart swell. It wasn't just because Waylon was giving Katy a precious gift of recognition. It was because he was so proud of his ability to consider someone else's feelings. He was compassionate. He was kind. As far as I was concerned, our social experiment was turning out just fine.

CHAPTER 31

My Mother-in-Law

WHEN DONNA KOONCE WENT into the hospital, I kept telling everyone that "Katy's mom" was having bypass surgery. I didn't want to give the state of Texas too much credit for recognizing my relationship to this extraordinary woman.

By the time Donna was moved to the ICU, I needed the shorthand of "mother-in-law." I spoke the words into the intercom, and the nurses buzzed me into the locked ward.

It felt strange to use a stuffy matrimonial label to describe Donna. She was terribly vain and would not abide any appellation that made her sound old. (Her own grandchildren were forbidden from using the dreaded "G" word.) Saying "mother-in-law" inevitably reminded me of our wedding and how Donna Koonce, grand Southern diva that she was, had interrupted the ceremony to ask everyone to "Look at that moon."

Eight years after our wedding, I was driving to the hospital in Lake Jackson. It was day six of Donna's stay. Her blood pressure had never returned to normal after the bypass and her vital organs were failing. The surgeon had offered the possibility of exploratory surgery, but cautioned that Donna was unlikely to survive another procedure. The family thoughtfully declined. Now the nurses said she wouldn't last another night.

I had taken Waylon to stay with friends and was anxious to rejoin Katy at Donna's bedside. Stuck at a stoplight, I felt something looming in my peripheral vision. The full moon. It was a spectacular golden dinner plate pasted on the sky. I texted my wife: "Look at that moon."

Back at the ICU, Katy held Donna's hand and told her about the beautiful spring moon. Then she spoke with the nurse. The doctor had given permission to stop the blood pressure medicine that was Donna's last artificial tie to life.

Katy stepped out of the room to call her brothers. It was the first time in six days that I'd been alone with Donna. With everyone else gone, I didn't feel self-conscious about taking her hand and putting my face next to her ear.

"Donna," I said, "it's Paige."

I had to try to project over the sound of the respirator. "Thank you for always being so sweet to me. Thank you for always loving Waylon like he was any other grandchild." I sobbed. And then, just as a wave of emotion was swelling inside me, I felt something equally strong and real emanating from Donna. Her presence was so strong, I was almost reeling, but I stood my ground and stayed in close.

"I learned so much from you," I said. My throat was tight with emotion. "It's Paige," I added. "I know you might not recognize my squeaky voice." But, even as I said it, I knew she knew me. "I love you and I'll miss you."

Still touching her arm, I sat back down on the stool by the bed. The fullness of her presence had subsided now, but I could feel it resonating inside me.

Katy came back from calling her brothers. She took her mother's hand. "I just called Phil and Blaine, Mommy. It's okay, you can let go if you need to." She kissed her mother and settled in to wait.

It was hard to look at Donna's beautiful face disfigured by swelling and tubes. We stared at the blood pressure monitor, which produced a new reading every 15 minutes. Katy busied herself by making sure her mom still had the crumpled tissue that she habitually clutched for comfort.

There was little sign of change until the heart monitor began to beep. We watched the lines on the screen grow slower and farther apart. Donna did not labor or rasp. Because she had a DNR order, the nurses walked calmly into the room. One put a stethoscope to Donna's chest. Then she handed it to the other. They agreed that the last heartbeat had happened at 12:13 a.m.

Except for the beeping of the heart monitor, the difference between life and death was barely evident. Then the nurses turned off the respirator and she was still. The respiratory therapist came and rolled the machine away.

I waited with Katy until her brother Phil arrived. Then I stepped outside to give them some time alone with their mama. Phil's wife was in the hallway and we made small talk. Donna was gone, but the intensity of our moment together was so great that she didn't feel all the way gone to me. The body in the room seemed insignificant now, because a small part of her spirit had migrated to my heart. I can still feel it right now, as I'm writing these words. It fills my chest and buoys me up.

Epilogue

MY FINAL MOMENT WITH Donna was the culmination of a long chain of experiences. From the Crystal Cove gift shop in Lily Dale to Dr. Berkson's clinic in the New Mexico desert, I had travelled far beyond my comfortable shell of suspicion and doubt. I bought a house based on good vibrations, learned I was pregnant from the electric touch of a would-be messiah, and strained to see the divine through the eyes of a young child. I emerged from Donna's hospital room with something real but amorphous: a jolt of connection surrounded by mystery.

Sometimes I think falling in love with Katy was the leap that launched this journey. But perhaps the impulse was already inside me and that's what drew me to her in the first place.

At times our love story threatened to eclipse what was happening inside me. A crisis can open your heart to the shared world of human suffering, but it can also send you scrambling for old habits of self-preservation and retreat.

It was only after the worst effects of Katy's treatment had passed that I started reserving Saturday afternoons for writing. So many ideas had been jostling around in my head, and at first I just wanted to write them down and arrange them for fun. But when I gave them light and space on the page, the ideas began to bloom into stories and the stories begged to be shared.

It was scary to reveal so much of myself, but it was also liberating. No more hoarding opinions and idiosyncrasies, no more hiding failures and disappointments.

Soon people started to tell me tales about their own weird and wonderful families. Queer people and straight people, cis people and trans people. Some said that moments from Waylon's childhood reminded them of their own childhood. Others recognized themselves in the mother who struggled to breastfeed or the partner who ran low on compassion. A few people said that they'd always wanted to be parents, but they had thought they were too queer, too trans, too damaged, too different. Now, they said, our story had inspired them to look beyond the two-dimensional LGBT poster families and to make family in their own way.

Like my final moment with Donna, all these precious moments of connection still buzz inside me. I hope that somehow—in some mysterious fashion that I respect but will never understand—they resonate in you too.

Acknowledgements

In 2007, when I wrote the first version of "Boygirls and Girlboys," Katy started saying that I should write a book. *Oh right,* I thought, *except I have no idea how to write a book and I work full-time and then there's Waylon and you and the laundry and I don't know when I would possibly find the time.*

In 2008, Katy inherited a sum of money that was almost exactly equal to my yearly salary at Soulforce. Instead of doing something sensible, like starting a retirement plan, Katy brought the money to me. "Quit your job," she said. "Write a book."

For the next two years, I taught part-time and spent the rest of my work days reading memoirs, taking long walks, and exploring narrative vistas and cul-de-sacs. I wrote some stories that would later become chapters, but mostly I just worked on becoming a better writer. It was an incredible luxury. I am beyond grateful for the financial support and, even more so, for Katy's confidence, which never dimmed even when it took me another seven years to complete this manuscript.

During this same period, I was lucky to have a brilliant and generous teacher. Abe Louise Young taught me to anchor my stories in concrete places and things. She didn't bat an eye when I started talking about writing a book, and her unwaning support and enthusiasm have sustained me through many crises of confidence and inspiration.

My friends Rachael Shannon and Gretchen Phillips gave me models of how to make a creative life. When they treated me like a fellow artist, it made me feel like the real deal. Rachael designed my beautiful book cover, AND her song "Dyke Hag" provided the inspiration for my title and the ethos for our whole way of life.

Bil Browning and Alex Bolinger gave me my first audience at *The Bilerico Project*, and *Bilerico* readers allowed me to imagine a readership for *Queer Rock Love*.

As a teacher and editor, Donna Johnson pushed me to go deeper and provided critical insights about memoir as a genre.

My sister, Kristen Schilt, provided valuable feedback on a very early draft and later invited me to read from my work in progress at the Center for Women and Gender Studies at the University of Chicago.

Scott Duane generously passed my manuscript to Zander Keig, who passed it on to Trystan Cotten and Max Valerio at Transgress Press. Their enthusiasm for the manuscript made me feel like I had found a home. I'm so proud to be a part of their activist publishing project.

John Cameron Mitchell provided literary inspiration and generously helped us secure crucial permissions. My hero!

Diane Anderson-Minshall offered thoughtful copy edits and helped me with consistent and inclusive language.

Christine Wicker's engrossing book *Lily Dale: The True Story of the Town that Talks to the Dead* helped me conjure the friendly ghosts of my first date with Katy. Another indispensable reference was *The Vigil: 26 Days in Crawford, Texas*, by W. Leon Smith and the staff of *The Lonestar Iconoclast*.

The book benefited immensely from a feedback session with Joanna Labow, Jen Margulies, Marcela Contreras, Katie Matlack, Aimee Thomas, Carrie Kinney, Jamie Harris, Kayla Floyd, Deb Campbell and Robin Czarnecki.

Silky Shoemaker was one of the book's last-minute angels.

Brian Trisel and Kathy Long allowed me to share a vulnerable moment in their lives. They are the most awesome donor family I can imagine.

I'd like to thank the Koonce family for having such a great sense of humor. I don't think I've told a single story about them that they didn't tell on themselves first. (Okay, maybe *one*.)

My parents, Alex Schilt and Charlotte McCluskey, taught me that girls can do anything. They are both excellent writers, and I'm grateful to have inherited their love of words.

Finally, Waylon Schilt-Koonce was my original muse. Thanks for giving me such good material and allowing me to share your stories. I love you!

In May 2015, Katy started taking Harvoni, a new med for hepatitis C. As of this writing, her viral load is undetectable.

32070750R00127

Made in the USA
Middletown, DE
21 May 2016